My Life in the Woods

My Life in the Woods

By Sidney Neal Greene

BOOKS

Copyright 2017 by Sidney Neal Greene. No portion of this book may be reproduced or transmitted in any form whatsoever without prior written permission from the publisher, except in the case of brief quotations published in articles and reviews.

ISBN 978-0-692-80508-4

Printed in the United States

an imprint of Pleasant Living Magazine LLC
www.pleasantlivingmagazine.com/books

To my son, *Caleb*

Table of Contents

Introduction	viii
A Special Day in the Woods	1
Amazing Insights into God's Creation	2
Wildlife Humor	3
In and Out	4
Funny But Painful	5
Traditional Archery	7
Hunting Dangerous Game	8
My First Deer Hunt	10
My First Fish and More as Told to Myself by Myself	13
Spring Turkey Season 2008	15
Do Turkeys Post a Lookout Bird?	18
More Turkey Hunting Adventures, Spring 2008	20
Bowser and the Bear	25
Live Bait for Smallmouth Bass, June 2009	27
A Great Bear Hunter	31
A Story from the Past	32
Believe It or Not	34
David's Fishing Story	35
Fishing for Avids	37
One Season – 2012	39
The Bear Who Was Afraid of a Turkey Decoy	43

Is It Wrong to Hunt?	45
Rabbits in the Snow	47
Striper Fishing, June 1996	49
The Legend of Falling Rocks	52
Tunnel Catfish with Allen and Jimmy Graham	55
Fishing with Roger – a Tribute	58
From the Past: Hunting the Ruffed Grouse	61
From the Past: Renegade Bear	63
From the Past: A Sad Bear Story	67
Carps	68
Chicken	70
Huntin' Stupid Deer	72
Living in Safer Times	74
Spot: A Great Coon Dog – Reminiscences from the Author and his Brother, Ronnie, Spot's Owner	78

Introduction

For several years, it has been on my mind to write stories about the great outdoors. I have always loved being outside. I remember, as a small boy, trying to follow my dad and my older brother through the woods carrying a little popgun. One day, I told my parents that I was going to take my popgun and go hunting, and so I headed out with our two dogs, Brownie and Ranger. I had gone about a quarter of a mile when the dogs ambushed a big groundhog. After they had killed it, I walked up to where the groundhog was and shot it several times—with my popgun. I picked the groundhog up by the tail and dragged him home. I went in the front door and proclaimed, "Look what I killed!"

A year or so later, I got my first BB gun. And I hate to admit it, but no bird, ground squirrel, or other small animal was safe when I was out with my gun.

The day came when I turned twelve years old and received my first shotgun. It was a Stevens single-barrel 16-gauge. I was scared to shoot it at first, but after I killed my first squirrel, there was no turning back. I killed fifty squirrels that first season, and we consumed every one that was not shot up too bad. I spent more time in the woods than doing my homework, and it showed up on my report card. In this and other cases, my dad would take my gun from me for a while, hoping that it would make me study. It never worked, and he never kept my gun more than a week or two.

In the wintertime, when there was a big snow, we all got together to hunt rabbits. Those were the days I will never forget. Dad and my brother, along with Uncle Lloyd, dad's brother, and his boys, loved when it snowed. One rabbit can make a lot of tracks in the snow going back and forth, up and down, and it was a challenge to try to track him.

Eventually, we would get a rabbit pinpointed, maybe in a briar patch, and someone would move in (all the while getting really torn up by the briars) and jump him up. A rabbit can be quite unpredictable as to which way he might run. They are very fast, and even with all those hunters waiting, the rabbit often got away.

In the summertime, we switched to fishing. My brother, my cousin, and I walked many a mile up and down Crane's Nest River and on Dotson Creek fishing for bass, redeyes, suckers, or anything that would bite.

Occasionally, we would all get together to go camping down on Cherokee Lake or Flannigan Dam. During those times, sitting around a campfire, I would listen to the men talk about their outdoor experiences from days gone by. Uncle Lloyd could tell such funny stories, they would nearly double us over. Other times, there would be more serious talk about God and the wonder of His creation. We all believed God created all things and gave us the outdoors to enjoy.

Now that I am retired, I want to spend some time writing about the great outdoors. I want to recount my experiences, along with the experiences and stories of other hunters and anglers, as well as exciting tales from the past and a few humorous narratives.

A few years back, I read a book called *The Great American Wild Turkey*, by Jack McDanielson. Mr. McDanielson taught anthropology at Washington and Lee University in Lexington, Virginia. In this remarkable book, he stated that he believes in evolution—that everything came into existence by chance. He talked about what a thrill it was to experience being outdoors and hunting turkeys. Many other authors have done this as well. I bring my stories to you from the standpoint of a Creator who gives us richly all things to enjoy. Our earth and every outdoor experience are the result of the kindness and goodness of God. The complexity of nature makes it absolutely impossible for it to be any other way. So go outside, into the fields and woods, and by the rivers and lakes, and find out for yourself the joy of being in the great outdoors.

A Special Day in the Woods

One day in mid-October, I was on a tree stand watching for deer. All around me, wildlife activity was going on. It was fascinating to watch squirrels in nearby trees, hanging upside down by their back feet, eating acorns. There were squirrels on the ground, chasing each other around and around and up and down the sides of trees. There were blue jays (jaybirds) chattering and ranting about those squirrels, who were apparently trespassing on their property. A ruffed grouse flew in and walked about ten feet before disappearing under a small holly bush. I never saw her again. How she managed to sneak off without me spotting her is beyond me.

Two little chipmunks made their appearance. I'll call them #1 and #2. They were playing a game of hide and seek: #1 would dive under a big rock or under a log; #2 would then search frantically until he located his pal. The chase would be on again. At one point, #1 tried to bury under some fallen leaves directly under my tree stand. Only the tip of his tail was protruding. #2 searched to and fro; a couple times, he scampered right on top of #1. Buried under the leaves, he did not move until #2 noticed the tail. He sneaked over and bit the end. Off they dashed again, dodging and chattering until they moved out of sight. I was so engrossed with these creatures that I never noticed if a deer came by or not.

Amazing Insights into God's Creation

Hunters and fishermen know how amazing the GPS unit is. You can put in the coordinates showing the exact location of a spot in the woods or on the water. You can leave and return to the exact spot with the GPS guidance system.

Consider the amazing sand wasp. It has a tiny brain about the size of a BB. The little female sand wasp tunnels into the sand on the beach and lays her eggs. She covers the entrance to the burrow with sand and flies away. She may fly as far as a mile down the beach looking for food. While she is gone, the wind blows sand around, further covering the entrance.

The little wasp returns, and miraculously, she can fly straight to the spot where her burrow is, move the sand from the entrance, and put in the food she gathered in the nest to feed her young. Her little brain computes several angles that come together to lead her to the exact spot where her little tunnel is. Did this come about by chance? Or is this the result of a wise, powerful Creator?

Wildlife Humor

Once there was a football game played between the big animals and the little animals. On the big animals team was an elephant, a rhinoceros, a lion, a giraffe, and others, all big and fast.

On the little animals team was a rabbit, an opossum, a chipmunk, a squirrel—you know, little animals.

On the first play, the big animals handed the ball to the elephant. He made it all the way to the end zone with all the little animals frantically trying to stop him. The game was a rout until the end of the first half.

When the second half started, the little animals had a new player—the centipede. The big animals had the ball first. The elephant took the handoff from the lion but was tackled in his tracks by the centipede. In the next play, the rhino tried running around the end on a sweep play, but was knocked down for a five-yard loss by the centipede. The lion went back to pass on the third down, but was sacked, yes, by the centipede.

The big animals punted the ball. The centipede caught the punt and ran the ball all the way back for a touchdown. The big animals were stopped again by the centipede and again he took the punt back all the way for another touchdown.

The game ended with the little animals leading by two touchdowns. The coaches met at midfield and shook hands. The coach of the big animals was amazed at the talent of the centipede. The coach exclaimed, "That centipede is the best football player that has ever lived! But where was he during the first half?" The coach of the little animals replied, "He was in the locker room, tying his shoes."

In and Out

Once there were two baby skunks that lived with their mom in a snug little den. Their names were In and Out, because In was always in and Out was always out.

But one day, Out was in and In was out. Momma skunk got worried because In was Out way too long. She told Out to go out and find In and bring him back in. So Out went out and in no time, Out came back in with In.

Momma skunk said, "Good job, Out. How did you find In so fast?" Out replied, "It was easy—In stinked."

Funny But Painful

The other day, I was inside my carpentry shop shooting my 243. I had a target set up about forty yards away. After a couple of shots, I made an adjustment to the scope and shot again. The adjustment brought the shot over where it should have been.

I took my ear protection off and then I saw an old stump sticking through the ice in a pond about two hundred yards away. I thought, I'll just try a shot at that old stump. I only had one more shell left. So without thinking, I loaded the last shell and let fly at the old stump.

Now remember, I was in my shop where I could get a good rest and hold the gun steady, so I rested it on an old coat on a workbench. As soon as I pulled the trigger, I remembered what I had forgotten to do—put my hearing protection back on. My whole body let me know about the mistake I had made. Obviously, my ears began ringing and my eyes were watering and just did not feel right. As a matter of fact, my stomach got upset, too. The blast from that little 243 inside my mostly metal building was awful!

That reminds me of a story that I read in a magazine about a deer hunter who shot at a deer using a 300 Remington Ultra Mag. He was hunting up in Canada for giant whitetail deer. The temperature got quite cold, often below zero. This hunter was in a box tree stand about six-by-six square, made of plywood, and there were little windows where he could watch for deer.

When he finally saw a big trophy come out into the field, he got excited and shot without first putting in his ear protection. Now, I think back on my own experience shooting the 243 inside my carpentry shop. My 243 is loud, but it sounds like a popgun next to a 300 Winchester Magnum. I remember when I shot one of these at my brother-in-law's house. I aimed at an old stump about three hundred yards away. Lying on the ground about ten feet below the stump was an old window. The blast from the 300 shattered the panes of glass in that old window.

Now, a 300 Winchester Magnum is loud and powerful, but it is not nearly as powerful as the 300 Weatherby and falls short of the power and noise blast of the 300 Remington Ultra. It is probably not funny, but I chuckle when I think of what this hunter went through when he fired his big 300 Ultra inside that little six-by-six tree stand.

What I have just written has been presented with some dry humor, but it is not really funny to lose your hearing from one blast of a gun, using a powersaw, or exposure to other loud equipment. I suffered for years from what a doctor called "shooter's ear." There was a constant ringing sound inside my left ear. It has mostly gone away, but occasionally I hear it. The simple obvious fact is that we need to wear some sort of good hearing protection. Eye protection is very important, too, as I have seen things happen that could very easily have damaged my eyesight. The woods and water would not be the same at all without being able to see and hear the things going on around you.

Traditional Archery

When we were growing up, trying to make a bow was a real passion. It was a contest between my friends and me to make the best bow. Most of our bows were made of a hickory tree limb. Finding a string was a big problem. Usually, we would use a piece of TV antenna wire. Making arrows was the biggest problem. We usually tried to whittle these out of sticks that were straight enough, but about all we could do was to cut a notch on one end and sharpen the other to a point. We tried using chicken feathers for fletching.

As I grew up, I never lost the dream of having a traditional bow. Over the years, I ordered some catalogs and was taken aback at the expense of the bows. So, again, I decided to make my own. I found a place that sold plans, materials, and instructions and settled on a takedown recurve. I had to make a laminating oven and molds to shape the limbs. The first bow I made was fashioned with a walnut riser with zebra wood laminated between strips of fiberglass, and I had an archery shop make me some carbon arrows with fletching.

Learning to shoot took a lot more practice than I thought it would. I do not use sights but shoot instinctively. During my first season, I missed two deer, but this year, I got two deer, a buck and a doe.

With all the modern archery of compound and crossbows, shooting a traditional bow offers a unique challenge. Judging distance was the hardest thing for me. I am still learning and always will be. I would rather be in the woods with my recurve than with a gun or compound bow.

Hunting Dangerous Game

Jack O'Connor and his guide and tracker were moving through the bush trying to locate a wounded tiger. Every sense was on full alert, knowing that up ahead the tiger was waiting. If the tiger charged, there would only be a few seconds to react before the tiger was upon them.

Such were my thoughts as I moved through the brush and briars following the tracks I had found in the snow. Sweat was dripping down my forehead and stinging my eyes even though the temperature was in the low teens.

I stopped to check my big double barrel to make sure it was loaded. There is nothing worse than finding out too late that you forgot to load your gun. There are tombstones in Africa, I am told, that have written on them, "I thought my gun was loaded."

I was breathing too hard and needed to try to relax and breathe more normally. After a few minutes, I moved on through the brush, following the tracks. My eyes and ears were watching and listening for movement or sounds. I would have even turned up my sense of smell if I could have.

A movement off to my right caused me to jerk around in that direction, my big double barrel ready to unload on it. It was just a little bird.

I cautiously moved on one step at a time. All of a sudden, there was an explosion directly in front of me. I only had a couple of seconds to shoot as the rabbit was running very fast and would quickly be out of range. I missed with the first barrel, but just as he was ducking under an old log, I unloaded the second barrel. I reloaded and moved cautiously forward, not knowing for sure if I had gotten him. He could be wounded and lying in wait only to run again.

He was there; I had hit him. I picked him up and turned around, then caught my size fourteen boot on a snag and down I went. I threw my gun in one direction and the rabbit in the other so my hands would be free to catch my fall. My shoulder brushed against a tree and my head barely missed a big rock on the way down. I got up and checked for broken bones or other injuries. I was lucky; everything was still intact. I retrieved my gun (both pieces of it) and my kill and began walking back towards home.

Jack O'Connor and his guide found their tiger without any mishap. The tiger was dead. I concluded that my rabbit hunt was far more dangerous than their tiger hunt.

I walked up the steps onto our porch and hung the rabbit up out of reach of our Great Dane puppy—who weighed 140 pounds! I stepped inside and my wife asked me, "Did you have a good trip?"

My First Deer Hunt

November 1974

I was in school, sitting at my desk in my senior English class, when a call came over the intercom for me to come to the office. My first thought was, "Oh no, what have I done?"

When I arrived at the office, I was pleasantly surprised to see my twenty-three-year-old brother waiting. He said that my dad had given permission to go on a deer hunt with my brother and his father-in-law.

Everything was ready to go. My license had been purchased, my shotgun was ready with buckshot and slugs, and sleeping bags and food were packed.

I didn't know what to think. It was totally unexpected. I hopped in the truck and we stopped to pick up Fred, my brother's father-in-law. We were going to hunt on a big farm up near Richmond, Virginia. My brother knew the owner and had gotten permission.

We arrived well after dark and set up our tent using the headlights of the truck. Man, it was cold, the temperature down in the teens. A full moon was out, making everything easy to see.

There was a huge cultivated cornfield, probably ten acres and bordered by swamps and thick brush.

The next morning we moved out, taking positions at the edge of the cornfield. After about an hour, I was so cold that I went back to camp to warm up. My brother and Fred were already there and had a good fire going.

We sat around the fire and talked about what each of us wanted to do, and after the sun came out, we headed out again. I chose to explore, looking for any deer sign, but I didn't really know what to look for. I didn't know about rubs and scrapes. I just picked out what I thought was a likely area and watched, and when nothing happened, I got up and moved on.

About 12:00, I headed back to camp for some lunch. My brother and Fred were already there, and none of us had seen a deer.

My brother had left his gun over in a corner of the cornfield. I am not sure why he did that. I volunteered to go get it for him. I left my gun at camp and walked across the field looking for the gun.

When I approached the area, a big doe was standing just a few yards from the gun. Doe season was in in that county; if I had brought my gun with me, I would have had an easy shot. After a dozen seconds or so, she hopped on off. I picked up my brother's gun and took it back to camp. I could have kicked myself.

That was the only deer any of us saw that day. The frustrating thing was that there were deer tracks everywhere.

The following day, we moved out before daylight and stayed all day. We packed our lunches. Again, neither of us saw any deer. We discussed it and decided that the deer were coming out only at night, probably because of the full moon. As we had only one more day to hunt, I decided I was going to take advantage of the moon. Visibility was very good; you could see all the way across the field. Since the deer were only coming out at night and making their way back into the swamp just before daylight, I decided I would be waiting for them at their well-used exit trial.

About 5:30 that morning, I took my sleeping bag and shotgun and crossed the field to a spot where there were a lot of tracks. It was very cold; the temperature was down in the teens. I got into my sleeping bag at the edge of the field and lay on my belly watching. I lay there looking at the skyline, memorizing every tree and tree limb .

All at once, I saw a flat-looking stick pointing up that was not there before. After a few seconds, the stick disappeared. A few more seconds later, a deer's head appeared, then the whole body. As I watched, an entire herd of deer emerged. There must have been at least twenty or more in the herd.

I moved my shotgun into position, wanting to shoot the lead deer, which was the largest. I was so excited that I moved a little too fast, and she saw my movement and stopped, staring at me. I then aimed at another large one. I pulled the trigger on my Stevens automatic shotgun, and the doe went down in her tracks.

What happened next is something that I will never forget. The herd of deer bolted at my shot, but a few seconds later, a huge buck appeared about thirty yards away. He just stood there like a big statue, looking back toward the downed deer. I believe that big buck had a nontypical rack that was easily over two hundred points. He looked like a big horse with antlers.

Here lies the biggest disappointment in all my years of fishing and hunting. My gun was practically already pointed at the big deer, but I could not shoot. My gun had jammed. I tried in vain to clear the spent shell out and get a new one in. After a full minute, the big deer whirled around and disappeared into the brush. Words cannot describe my disappointment, but at least I had gotten a doe. The doe was quite large; she dressed out at over 150 pounds, but compared to the buck, she was very small. I slung her over my shoulder and carried her across the field, about a half-mile walk, without stopping. I had not even bothered to gut her, as I did not know how. My brother and Fred were excited for me and were amazed that I had carried the deer that far by myself.

The following day, we hunted half a day, but none of us had any luck. The final day was Thanksgiving, so we headed back home to celebrate and give thanks. I am still disappointed at not getting the big buck. What I know now is if I had waited until the herd had passed on, the big buck was following and I would definitely have gotten a shot at him. Of course, if my gun had not jammed, I would have gotten him. Since that day, I have killed several deer, but none were even half as big as that monster.

My First Fish and More As Told to Myself by Myself

Summertime, 1963
7 years old
Purpose in life: To catch a fish out of the creek by our house
Overwhelming problem: No hook, no fishing line, no pole
How problem was solved: Used stickpin bent into a curve for hook
Line was a piece of mom's sewing thread. (Used white thread. Red, yellow, blue, and other colors seemed to scare the fish away.) Pole was an old broomstick.

After I got my fishing tackle together, I dug up grass below my house to find worms. Took a while to find a couple. Walked down to the creek where there was a big rock in the middle of the creek. Fish were under rock: small silversides and hornyheads.

After baiting hook, I let it sink to the bottom. Water was about two feet deep. After a little while, line started to move very slowly. Pulled up on line; something was jerking. Pulled up very slowly. Huge crawdad, about three inches long, very black, holding on with his pinchers. Let crawdad down. He let go and backed back into the water.

Time: Next day
Bait: More worms dug up
Water clarity: Water clearer than day before. Little fish grabbing at bait.
Problem: Could not catch a fish because "hook" was too big for the size of fish attacking bait

After long moments of waiting, I finally hooked a big one. It got off because of barbless stickpin. After analyzing the problem, I decided on a remedy. The next time a fish big enough to get his mouth over the hook came along, I would jerk very hard to land him.

I put my line in the water and watched as the little fish took turns attacking my bait. They quickly learned how to pull the worm off. After losing a couple worms, I broke the worm into pieces and put just a small piece on the hook.

I watched and finally saw a big three-incher get the hook in his mouth. I gave a mighty jerk, and the fish was catapulted out of the water and went flying straight up into the air. On the way back down, he briefly got caught on some tree limbs before he finally landed about ten feet away. I had brought a tin can with me to put my fish in, in case I caught one.

I walked over, picked him up, and put him in my livewell.

Earlier in life, I had built a little pond in our yard by building a little dam in another little creek running near our front yard. I had dreams of stocking it. When I added him to my pond, my fish had unfortunately not survived his trip through the air and just floated belly up.

Before I had time to go fishing again to restock my pond, I added a couple of crawdads. Soon after this, it rained and destroyed my little fishpond.

Spring Turkey Season 2008

This year's spring turkey season was the most interesting one that I can remember. It was full of action, experiences, close calls, and misses. It makes for a unique story for those who like to hunt. After a quick quote from a favorite writer and a little hunting background, I'll tell you what happened on opening day.

"The wild turkey provides the greatest challenge that upland hunting offers. No other upland bird is as strong, fast, elusive, tough, wary, or clever. The difficulty inherent in killing a mature gobbler is sobering." (John McDaniel, *The American Wild Turkey*)

My name is Neal Greene, and I live in southwest Virginia near a little town called Pound. I have hunted and fished since I was old enough to keep up with my dad. We spent many a day tracking through the woods, hunting mostly squirrels and rabbits. During the 1960s through about 1990, that was all the game there was locally. Now, we have deer, bears, and turkeys in abundance.

My favorite of these is hunting gobblers during the spring season. I got my first big tom in 2001. He weighed nineteen pounds and had an eleven-inch beard. On the last day of the season, I bagged another one that weighed twenty pounds and had an eleven-and-a-half-inch beard.

On the opening day of the 2008 spring turkey season, I got up at 4:30 a.m., ate a little breakfast, and drove out to my hunting site. On the drive over, I set a personal goal to fill my three tags during that season.

I drove off onto an old coal-mining strip job and parked my truck. There is an old logging road coming up out of the woods, and I walked down the road as quietly as I could. I knew there were turkeys around as I had seen a lot of scratching during preseason scouting. I actually got there a little bit too late, as it was almost daylight. My plan was to move in quietly and just listen for gobbling.

I had not walked a hundred yards when some roosting hens flushed out and flew off. I moved on down the road and sat on the ground with my back against a tree. It was not very long until I heard the first turkey gobble. Almost immediately, turkeys began gobbling from every direction. I made a few yelps on my Cane Creek turkey caller. Immediately, a tom answered. He was not more than a hundred yards away, so I felt confident that I could call him in. I remembered the hens that had flushed during my walk in. I was sure that the gobbler expected these hens to come to him. I figured that if they did not come in, he would eventually go to them.

I sat there for forty-five minutes making occasional soft calls and scratching in the leaves. The gobbler would answer every time. I do not ever remember hearing a turkey gobble so much! It was obvious that this turkey was not going to leave his strutting zone. He was not going to move until the hens came in to him. Maybe he knew that they had flown off the roost and expected them soon.

Anybody that has done much turkey hunting knows that it involves making a lot of decisions. Should I sit still and wait? Should I get up and move? In this case, I was awfully close to this turkey, and if I moved around, there was a good chance I would be spotted. If I waited too long, the hens might go to him, and the flock would move off.

I decided that I would go after him. My plan was to keep calling and scratching in the leaves as I made my way. I had to climb a very steep hill, and the tom was up on top on a flat area. My fear was that he would come over to the edge and see me. I managed to get to within ten yards of the top of the ridge and hid behind a tree.

I made a couple of high-pitched soft calls to try to get him to come over to the edge where I could get a shot. That turkey would respond with loud gobbles and move in my direction, but would not come to the edge. I scratched some more, and he would answer, but he would not come close enough for me to see him.

I decided to take a chance and move up to the top of the ridge to where I could look out over the flat he was on. Now, this turkey was not more than thirty or forty yards away, and I knew he would hear me walking, as the leaves were very dry and the hill very steep. I got down on my hands and knees and began crawling. I again tried to imitate a turkey scratching as I sneaked closer. I would move the leaves away, making myself a path, as I moved very slowly. Tom evidently thought a hen was moving in as he kept gobbling. I had picked out a big tree that I could move up behind. I made it to the tree and stood without spooking the gobbler.

There is nothing more exciting than to be close to a big tom, knowing that any second, you will see him. I slowly moved my head and peered around the tree. I had my gun up to my shoulder and my finger on the trigger.

I was hunting with the same gun I deer hunt with, a Remington Model 700 243. I had killed turkeys with it before. I only own two shotguns: one is a 20-gauge double barrel, which I did not have confidence in; the other is a single barrel 12-gauge (made in Korea) which, I found out from experience, was not a turkey gun. So......, I peeped around the tree, looking through the scope. Sure enough, there he was about twenty-five yards away. At first, all I could see was his tail feathers. I could not see his head or chest as they were blocked by a tree. I stood still, and after a few seconds, he moved forward a few steps. He looked right at me though I had not moved. I put the crosshairs on his chest and pulled the trigger.

You should have seen the feathers fly. They all flew in one direction, since they were still permanently attached to the turkey. I could not believe that I had missed! Very disappointed, I walked over to check things out. I found that the bullet had grazed a small tree about two feet from where the turkey had been.

Obviously, it was a big letdown to work so hard and get that close only to miss, but that is turkey hunting. It was not the first time nor would it be the season's last.

Do Turkeys Post a Lookout Bird?
(Continued from Spring Turkey Season 2008)

In his book, *The American Wild Turkey,* John McDaniel insists that turkeys should be hunted with a shotgun only. In his opinion, it is not sporting to use a rifle. In Kentucky, shotguns only are allowed.

In my experience with turkey hunting, I have had occasions when I needed a different gun than the one I was carrying. I suppose that everyone who has hunted can say this. If I had had a shotgun in this next adventure, there is no doubt that I would have gotten this turkey. I had debated in my mind, "Should I buy a good shotgun or keep carrying my 243?"

While walking out of the woods that opening day morning, my initial disappointment of missing that big gobbler had worn off. To me, there is nothing like the sound of a wild gobbler; this turkey would live to gobble and strut around again. It was like "catch and release" in fishing. I had gotten within twenty yards of a bird that has the sharpest sense of hearing and sight. Anytime a hunter can do that, even if the turkey gets away, he has had a successful hunt.

A couple days later, I woke very early and was in the woods before daylight. I made my way as quietly as I could and got in a position above where he had roosted. Daylight came, and distant turkeys started gobbling. Nothing happened, though, where I was. The gobbler had changed his roosting site. He didn't roost in this site again that season.

Turkeys were gobbling on another ridge about three hundred yards away. I moved over in the direction of that same tom turkey, and when I got as close as I dared, I sat down and did some soft calling. He answered immediately but would not leave the flock he was with.

After a while, he gobbled but was even farther away. The hens had gotten nervous and were moving away and taking him with them. I got up and moved, circling around in the direction they were moving, and I found a good spot to hide and watch. For twenty minutes, I sat and watched.

All of a sudden, the gobbler sounded off. For some strange reason, the turkeys had again changed direction. Now, they were actually moving back in the direction from which I had first called them in. Now, every time I made a call, the gobbler would answer.

One of my favorite hunting maneuvers is to try to follow a moving flock. It very seldom works, but I like the challenge of trying. After all, the excitement of turkey hunting is in the trying.

I began to move in their direction, occasionally calling and scratching in the leaves. I worked my way around until I was about one hundred yards from the flock, when I got busted. A lone turkey was in a tree and blasted a warning call. Off he flew to the flock. The entire group moved off in a hurry, and I had no idea where they went.

The question arose in my mind, "Do turkeys post a lookout bird? Or did this bird just happen to be there?" From my experiences throughout the rest of the season, I now know that they do.

More Turkey Hunting Adventures, Spring 2008

Some coon-hunting friends of mine told me about an area where they had found a lot of turkey signs. I was up at 3:30 the next morning as I had a long walk to get there. I drove my truck through the wood up an old logging road. Although there is a four-wheeler trail that goes off down the mountain and up the other side, I do not own a four-wheeler, so I had to walk in. This country is very rough and steep, and if not for the four-wheeler trail, I would have had quite a hard time getting there.

It was daylight before I got to the area, and I really didn't know what to expect when I arrived. A turkey started gobbling, and I listened for a while and decided to get closer. As I moved in, I stopped occasionally to call, and he answered every time. I had gotten about one hundred yards from him and decided to move over to a big oak tree and sit down. I was moving as quietly as possible and trying to keep in a hidden position. All at once, I heard a warning call. A turkey resting on the limb of an old fallen tree saw me. It was as if she was watching for me like a sentry, While chirping a warning call, she immediately flew off. The flock fled and I never heard the gobbler again.

I spent the rest of the morning just scouting around and saw a lot of scratching, so the next morning found me back again. I left even earlier so I would be there before daylight. Anxiously, I sat down and waited for light to come to see what would happen.

There was not much gobbling going on this morning. Occasionally, I would hear a tom off on another ridge, but nothing close by. Somewhere near 9:00, a turkey started gobbling about two hundred yards below me. I called to him and he answered. My vision was hindered by rhododendron and ivy, so I carefully moved a bit farther away, but with a better view and sat up against a big poplar tree. I had three calls with me: two slate calls, one from Knight & Hale, one from Cane Creek, and a small box call. I started off with a course of yelps on my Knight & Hale. The tom gobbled immediately. Purring and more yelping calls came next, varying among high, medium, and low pitches. All calls were soft and nonaggressive. I reached over and scratched in some leaves to further get his attention. I have found that a turkey usually makes a series of three scratches followed by a rest. That is what I did, too.

After just a few minutes, I saw him, and his girlfriend, too! She was plain, but Tom was the most beautiful bird I had ever seen. His head and entire chest were bright red, really more like a bright orange. He was an absolute trophy because of this unusual coloring. Now, I was completely camouflaged with gloves and a face covering. I had my gun on my shoulder and across my knee, pointed in his direction. I never moved at all. About forty yards away, the hen stopped. She was looking directly at me and was suspicious. She started to move away, but Tom didn't want to follow. She clucked and darted about, wanting him to leave. Tom wanted to stay and find all the other girls he had heard. She clucked some more and urged him to follow her. He kept anxiously pacing around and wouldn't stop, even for one second. Here was another situation in which I needed a shotgun rather than the 243. During this entire display, I kept following Tom with the scope's crosshairs waiting for him to stop. He became more and more nervous. I had better shoot quick.

When Tom temporarily vanished behind a big poplar tree, I committed myself to shoot when he came out the other side. I thought I was right on him, but just as I pulled the trigger, he only slightly dipped his back. Once again, the feathers flew. This time there were two bunches. One went east and the other went west. All feathers were still attached to their respective owners.

I got up and moved off in the direction the hen had flown. I was hoping to lure Tom back in. I called, using the "lonesome hen" yelp for another hour, but never saw or heard from Tom again.

Disappointed, I got up and started out of the woods as I had a rather long walk back to the truck. My thoughts were, "I'm never going to use my 243 again! From now on, I'll bring my double barrel 20 gauge."

On the way out, I changed my mind about quitting and moved off in another direction. I happened upon some fresh scratching from a flock of turkeys feeding on an old mining strip job shelf around the side of a mountain. Above it was a similar shelf. I scrambled up the ledge and started to mimic a feeding turkey by scratching in the leaves. After traveling along about three hundred yards, I saw the flock on the lower shelf about a hundred yards away. The flock saw me too and began moving off. One young gobbler didn't move quite fast enough, and I made a perfect shot on him. The 243, which was the wrong gun earlier, was just right for this shot. You just never know. The bullet hit him right where his neck joined his body and did very little damage. He probably weighed about fifteen pounds, but felt like fifty by the time I got him back to the truck. He certainly was a long way from being my "Tom Trophy," but he was perfect to put in the oven.

A few days later, I went back to the area where I had hunted on opening day. I wanted to see if Tom or the one I now thought of as "Old Lucky" was still around. I expected him to be gobbling again and was not disappointed. He was now on private land with a bunch of hens and would not answer my calls. I did pass up a shot on a nearby young jake.

Five o'clock the next morning found me walking the same four-wheeler trail, hoping I might again see the old orange-chested tom. I waited in the area where I had encountered him, but he never gobbled or responded in any way to my calling.

The following dawn, I was back again and a turkey began gobbling about a half mile away. I sneaked along the trail and came out near some gas wells. The gobbler was a couple hundred yards down the mountain hollering his head off. I thought, "This is going to be an easy one." Sure, it would.

I moved in his direction and got set up to call him in. Instead of responding to my calls, he suddenly grew quiet. The next time I heard him, he had moved down the mountain, crossed a creek and was traveling up the other side of the mountain.

The area was very steep and rough, covered with ivy and rhododendron. I figured he was hurrying to join a flock of hens, so I decided to go after him. I made my way down off the steep hillside, ducking under the brush and slipping and sliding along until I, too, crossed the creek and started up the other side.

I made a really soft call, and he answered about two hundred yards away. I began to slowly move in his direction, scratching in the leaves as one of his hens would. I got to within fifty yards of him but could not see him.

He quit gobbling. I waited a long ten minutes. Maybe I should make my way on up. Yes. I was mostly just crawling on my hands and knees, calling only occasionally.

All at once, in the tree above me, I heard the "cluck, cluck, cluck" of a turkey. The big gobbler had hopped up in this tree and was watching the trail he had just walked. I'm pretty sure he had me in his crosshairs the entire time but waited until I was right under him before announcing my arrival. I'm sure his "cluck, cluck, cluck" was really a "hey, hey, hey!" as he heehawed at my turkey tactics. He flew off in the direction I had first heard him.

I wandered on up to the top of the mountain and met up with two other turkey hunters. They, too, had been working the same turkey, yet from above him. They didn't know where he had disappeared to, and I didn't tell them. We talked about him a while and agreed that he was a wise old tom. He had been hunted a lot and would be hard to kill. He sure had put one over on me.

The hunters asked me how I had gotten there, and I told them that I had walked in and pointed in the direction in which my truck stood. They looked at me in disbelief that I had walked so far. They had driven in; their truck was only a couple hundred yards away. Well, I didn't know you could drive in that close. I had come to enjoy the walk and had lost some weight. I spent another couple hours exploring, and as I came back to the truck, I heard the "Old Wise Man" (the name I gave him) gobbling. It was about one o'clock in the afternoon. I sure hadn't expected to hear him again that day.

I set up above him and began calling with all three calls and scratching the leaves. His gobbles grew silent, but I heard him moving around and knew he was coming in. About ten minutes passed and I heard him right behind me! I moved my head around very slowly, and there he was about twenty feet away, looking me straight in the eye. Here was the Old Wise Man. He, too, was a beautiful bird with a red head and neck. I knew I would not be able to get a shot off with the

243, so I just jumped up and ran after him. I noticed a look of frozen bewilderment because he hesitated and I came within ten feet of him before he flew. I counted it as a victory having gotten that close to this bird.

A couple days later, I was back on the last day of the season. Sure enough, he was there close by and gobbling. Again, as soon as I started calling, he grew quiet. I sat waiting and watching. And waiting and watching. And waiting…YAWN! A young jake came in, and with an easy shot, ended my season. I never saw or heard the Old Wise Man again that day, but I expected he—and I—will be back.

Bowser and the Bear
By Jeanette Stapleton, my late aunt

When I was a girl, my grandparents used to tell ghost stories and animal adventures. One story goes like this:

There was this farm where a man and his wife and their twelve-year-old son lived. The boy's name was Bowser. One day mom told Bowser to take the day off from working on the farm and go down to the river and catch a mess of fish.

Bowser was well pleased to do this chore. He got his cane pole and a can of worms and was about to set off when his mom told him he should take a rifle, as there were bears and panthers around.

Bowser made his way down to the river and saw a large tree that had fallen into the water. He leaned his gun against a tree and walked out on the tree to fish.

The fishing was good and he soon had a stringer of redeyes. He had been so intent on his fishing that he had failed to keep an eye out. He paused in his fishing and looked around. What he saw terrified him. There on the bank watching him stood a huge black bear. The bear had smelled Bowser's fish and came to have a meal of Bowser's fish.

Bowser stared at the bear and the bear stared back without fear that bears normally have for humans. This bear was so big he was not in fear of anything. He was king of his territory, and Bowser was an intruder.

Bowser saw his gun leaning against the tree and wished there was some way he could get at it. He was trapped until his father and mother got worried about him and came to find him.

He just stood there watching the bear and the bear stared back. Suddenly the bear got up and walked down to the log. He slowly moved along the log toward Bowser. When the bear was almost on top of him, Bowser flung the stringer of fish in the bear's face. The bear snapped at the fish and in so doing, lost his balance and fell off the log into the river.

Bowser ran down the log and picked up his gun. The bear was attempting to climb back onto the log when Bowser shot him. The bear fell back into the river and the current carried him down, where he lodged on a sandbar.

Bowser ran home as fast as his legs could carry him. His dad was coming in from the field. Bowser told his dad what happened. They reloaded the gun and walked down to the river. The bear was still there. He was so big, they had to use a team of horses to pull him out.

Word got out about the bear, and neighbors came to see it. Everyone agreed it was the biggest bear they had seen. They bragged about Bowser's bravery and how he had reacted in this situation.

Live Bait for Smallmouth Bass, June 2009

Fishing for smallmouth bass is very exciting. I have had some great trips catching one three-to-four pounder after another. I remember one fall day when fishing with my son, Caleb, who was about ten years old at the time. We fished for a couple of hours without having any action, so we moved to a very unlikely looking spot. My plan was to fish there for a few minutes and move on. You can't always tell by just looking at a spot whether there are fish there. I was in the front of the boat and was in the process of baiting my hook with a sucker minnow. In my experience, sucker minnows are the best live bait to use, especially in the late fall.

Caleb was fishing with a Blueback Sassy Shad. I was watching when his rod jerked down very hard. He fought the fish up to the boat, and he had hooked a smallmouth bass in the three-and-a-half to four-pound range. Before I could reach out and grasp the fish by his lower jaw, the hook pulled loose and the fish was gone. I hardly ever keep a smallmouth unless the fish has injured itself and is bleeding.

We anchored the boat and for about an hour we caught smallmouth—one after another. All the fish were over fifteen inches long.

On another fishing trip, a friend of mine, named Danny, was with me. I had caught a bunch of sucker minnows for bait. I baited up with the largest minnow we had, about six inches long, and made a long cast. We were fishing on a rocky point at the two-mile marker on Boone Lake. In less than a minute, I had one on. He came to the top of the water and just kind of plowed around on the surface. He must not have been hooked very well, so he pulled loose. He definitely was a trophy fish weighing in the five-pound range.

For about an hour we caught at least ten nice smallmouth. The weather turned bad with high winds and we had to get off the lake.

I would rather use artificial lures for smallmouth. Sometimes though, live bait will catch fish when artificial bait will not. In the summer months up into late fall, smallmouth love crawfish—or "crawdads" as we always called them.

The best way to catch crawdads is to use a minnow net, which works especially well in the daytime. You can make one using a wire clothes hanger. Bend the wire into a six-inch by eight-inch oval and attach something like an old thin curtain or door screen so the water can run through it easily. Find a creek that has lots of crawdads. Sometimes they are out in the open. If you try to grab them by hand, they will shoot off backwards into deep water. The trick is to move slowly, getting behind the crawdad. Bring the net down behind him, then put a stick or your hand in front of him. This will make him dart off backwards, straight into your homemade net.

My ten-year-old niece went with me once to catch crawdads. I had a net; she was just using her hands. I thought I was doing pretty good, definitely better than she was. We stopped after about one-half hour to compare our catches. She had caught three times more than I had. This just shows what quick little hands can do.

The very best way to catch crawdads is to hunt at night. Use a flashlight to spot them. They come out at night to feed. If you shine your light directly on them, they usually will not move. Just reach down and pick them up.

On one trip, my son and I made it over to Pound Lake that has both large and smallmouth bass. We caught about three-dozen crawdads for bait. Smallmouth are really looking for crawdads from summer up to late fall, when the water cools down and the crawdads move into deeper water and hide under rocks or holes on the lake bottom.

We were in the dog days of August. The water was warm and clear, making for tough fishing during the day. We fished for about two hours and were about out of bait. We had caught nine smallmouths and two largemouths, all within sight of the launch ramp. There was only one crawdad left. We moved over to the boat ramp, waiting our turn to load our boat.

I made a long cast parallel to the shore in about ten feet of water. Before the crawdad reached the bottom, the line started moving out. I set the hook and felt the weight of a large fish. I had four-pound test line on and had to play the fish very carefully. After about five minutes, I got the fish to the boat and reached out and grabbed the fish by the lower jaw. People on the bank were watching and were amazed almost as much as I was. It was a big fat smallmouth, twenty-one inches long. That was the first smallmouth I had ever caught that was over four pounds. I put him in the livewell, where there was plenty of oxygen. After about five minutes, he was ready to be released.

On another summer evening, my brother and I were fishing top water lures for strippers, making long casts toward the bank and working the lures slowly back to the boat. My brother had already caught a sixteen-pound stripper, the largest fish he had ever caught. I was using a nine-inch Redfin and made a cast that landed the Redfin about two feet from the bank. I let the waves go away and started reeling the lure. It had not moved a foot when it was smashed really hard. It had to be a big smallmouth.

I was using seventeen-pound test, but it was all I could do to control the fish. It put up the most spectacular fight of any fish I had ever caught. He stayed on the surface thrashing, making splendid jumps, and tail-walking like crazy. When I got him over to the boat, he dived down as fast and as hard as he could. I thought he was going to break my line. When I got him back up, the fight was gone out of him. I put him in the livewell hoping he would revive in the oxygen-rich water. After a few minutes, I checked on him. He was lying belly up. The fish had literally fought himself to death. He measured nineteen inches long and was close to four pounds.

When using live bait, a fish sometimes swallows the bait and you cannot get the hook out. For this reason, I use wire hooks no larger than a #10. This way the fish can be released without harming them. I cut the line and turn a fish loose if I don't want to keep it. You will probably lose more fish using smaller hooks, but you should get more bites.

One night, I was tied up to an old pine tree that had fallen in the lake. There are some really big crappies in this lake. I had brought along some creek minnows I had seined, thinking that bigger bait would attract bigger fish. It was the middle of August, and the katydids were chirping very loudly that night. I love to fish at night, especially when katydids are chirping. I had two lanterns hanging over the side of the boat. I was using #14 hooks and six-pound test line. I hooked and landed two of the biggest largemouth bass I had ever caught. Both were over twenty inches. I also caught three crappies thirteen to fifteen inches in length.

This story took place during the dog days of summer, when catching bass on any lure is difficult, but catching and using live bait seems to be more effective and is certainly more fun.

A Great Bear Hunter

There was an old man who lived in a cabin in the woods with his wife. The old man was reputed to have been a great bear hunter in his younger days. He never missed a chance to brag about his exploits either. He talked about how he would love to go on one more bear hunt before he died.

The old man and his wife had two grandsons who came to visit for a week, and he entertained them with his hunting adventures. He sat in his wheelchair and looked longingly over the mountains surrounding his cabin and said, "If only I could go on one more hunt."

His grandsons talked it over and offered to take grandpa on a bear hunt by pushing him around in his wheelchair.

They got their gear together, gave grandpa his gun, and they started off pushing the wheelchair.

They had bumped along for nearly an hour when a great big bear appeared and stood up on his hind legs and let out a big roar.

The two grandsons left grandpa with the bear and ran for home as fast as their legs would carry them.

They saw grandma and started yelling, "Grandma, Grandma! Grandpa just got ate by a big bear!

Grandma retorted, "What are y'uns talkin about? He got here five minutes ago."

A Story from the Past

There is a growing anti-hunting sentiment in this country. There are organizations such as PETA that would have all hunting outlawed. But this story is not to argue the pros and cons of this sentiment. The fact is that man has depended on the killing of animals for thousands of years. During the antediluvian period, man was strictly a vegetarian. But when Noah and his family got off the ark, God told Noah in Genesis, chapter 9, verses 2 and 3, "And the fear of you and the dread of you shall be upon every beast of the earth, and upon every fowl of the air, upon all that moves upon the earth and upon all the fishes of the sea. Every moving thing that lives shall be meat for you."

Since that time, man has had to kill animals for his survival. He could no longer make it as a vegetarian. Our nation's Native Americans had to kill to survive; they ate the meat and used the skins for shelter and for clothing.

My dad was born in 1918, and his family had no electricity. During spring and summer, they worked hard raising corn, beans, and potatoes. They would gather walnuts in the fall and keep their barn stall full of fruits and vegetables.

For their meat, they depended mainly on rabbits and squirrels, as there were no deer or other big game around. Dad loved to tell stories of their days hunting rabbits in the snow. He said that big snow was always welcome. He and his brothers, cousins, and friends would meet and track down rabbits. Most of them did not have a gun. Their game plan was to catch as many as they could strictly by using their hands. Rabbits were plentiful, but they never sat out in the open; they stayed holed up under big rocks or in rockbars, large areas of land that "grow" rocks.

When the men tracked a rabbit to a hole, they would turn a

ferret in to run the rabbit out. If hunting a rockbar, they never knew where the rabbit would come out. The hunters would kneel down at a possible exit hole and try to catch the animal, and sometimes, there would be more than one rabbit in the hole.

Dad told a story about his cousin, Whitely, who was very good at this task. One time, three rabbits fled the hole where Whitely was waiting, and he caught all three of them! He had one in each hand and one pinned between his stomach and knees. The rabbits were kicking and squealing, and Whitely was cussing like a sailor. After the guffawing slacked, the young men came to his aid.

Dad said Whitely loved to hunt rabbits above all else. When there was a new snow on the ground, you could always count on him being there ready to go. He never carried a gun or owned any boots. He wrapped his feet in grass sacks and rags, which were tied onto his feet with more strips of rags. Just before rabbit season in 1930, Whitely died. A few weeks later, my dad and his brother, Lloyd, were visiting Whitely's grave. There was fresh snow and a rabbit had hopped across the grave. Dad and Lloyd were quiet for a while, sadly looking at the grave and remembering how much Whitely loved to rabbit hunt. Finally, Lloyd said, "It's rabbit time—Whitely's rabbit time."

And so, they went hunting.

Believe It or Not

The following fishing story might or might not have happened. After reading this story, think it over, and you decide.

I was told about a fishing trip that took place about forty or fifty years ago. Some men went on a camping trip down on Cherokee Lake. They got there after dark and carried their gear down to the lake.

One of the men had never fished before. His fishing rod was homemade—made out of a hickory pole about eight or ten feet long. He had put handmade guides on it and had a big reel that would hold three hundred yards of twenty-pound test, at least. His sinker was a big piece of lead that probably weighed three or four ounces. That was so he could "cast out where the biggins lived," he said.

After baiting his hook with a big gob of chicken liver, he gave the rod a mighty heave. The story goes that the other fishermen were amazed at how far his cast went. The line kept going on and on and on. Nobody even heard it hit the water.

About an hour later, his line started moving out—very fast.

After fighting what everyone thought must be a real big one, he dragged out a big ole possum The possum was very mad and attacked the first man he saw. It took all of them working together to get control of the possum and cut him loose. Evidently, the bait had traveled all the way across to the other side of the lake, where the possum had found it.

David's Fishing Story

Written by my 11-year-old nephew

It was on a Saturday evening and my little brother, our papaw, and his brother were on Cherokee Lake fishing for striped bass and catfish. We had been fishing for about two hours when we were hit by a big storm. Our boat washed up on the shore, so my papaw tied it to a boulder. After my papaw tied the boat up, we saw a house. We went to see if anybody was home so that we could get out of the rain until it stopped. When we got to the house, we saw a lady. We knocked on the door and the lady saw us, but she did not answer the door. My papaw said she called the police because she was scared. We then headed across a field and found some trees to sit under until the terrible rainstorm quit.

Finally, after a long and wet half hour, the rainstorm stopped, so we headed back to the boat and started fishing again. It was about ten o'clock at night, and at that time, we had been fishing for four hours, except for the time of the storm. We were fishing by an island when I hooked a big fish. Papaw thought it had to be a twenty-pound striper and told me to hold on tight to the rod and reel. I fought the fish, and it pulled our boat into the wind where we launched, which was about one to one-and-one-half miles away. It took me a good forty-five minutes to get the fish in. What took my papaw by surprise was what kind of fish it was and why it fought the way it did. It was a blue catfish.

We took the catfish home to eat, but before we skinned it, we figured its weight by squaring the length and girth and adding them together and dividing this by eight hundred, and we ended up with 19.4 pounds. This was twenty-four hours after we got it out of the water, so its weight would have decreased quite a bit. We also got some pictures of me with the catfish.

One day my papaw decided to put me in the Tennessee hunting and fishing book. The man we talked to said the catfish probably weighed twenty-two pounds when we got it out of the water. When we were fishing, I was real excited because I am a true fisherman and would stay up for ten days and fish if I could. I have been fishing since I was three, so pretty much my whole life. Fishing is my passion, and I would never turn down a fishing trip no matter where or what time of the year it is.

Fishing for Avids

On Tuesday, March 24, 2009, I happened to be in a sporting goods store, and while browsing around, I overheard a conversation between two customers. I only remember a couple of things they said. One gentleman stated that he was an avid fisherman, and his favorite lake to fish in was… I better not disclose the name of the lake because Mr. Avid Fisherman might not want me to tell his secret.

Now, I've caught many kinds of fish, including carp, stripers, smallmouth and largemouth bass, suckers, bluegills, hornyheads, red eyes, silversides, and hogmollies (not necessarily in that order), but I've never caught an avid. About a week later, I decided to go try to catch one. I didn't know what avids liked to eat, so I just bought some crappy minnows.

My wife and I headed out for the above secret lake, launched our boat, and I decided to fish around the launch ramp. I checked the water temperature and found that the surface temp was 48 degrees and, at twenty feet, it was 42 degrees. I recorded this information and everything else we did in case we found avids, especially if we had good luck. I could then say, "We found them in twenty feet of water on the edge of a drop off at the mouth of a cave."

We fished and fished; or I fished and fished—my wife chose to read a book. After not getting a bite, I decided to ask the only two other people on the lake if they knew anything about avid fishing. They laughed like I had just told a hilarious joke, and one held up a salamander they had just caught.

The only excitement we had that day was when I snagged a tree limb. At first it felt like I had one on. After untangling my line from the tree limb, I released it.

We decided to call it a day, not having gotten one real bite. My excuse (what fisherman doesn't have one?) was that the water wasn't the right color and too cold. Later in the week, someone told me that avids live on land and do not come out until late at night.

Anyway, I quickly lost interest in being an avid fisherman and decided that catching suckers in a nearby creek was much more fun.

One Season – 2012

The 2012 turkey season had some good experiences and one really bad one. The season opened on Saturday, April 14, for gobblers. The number of gobblers allowed was three. I've never personally filled my tags, but every year, I keep this goal in mind.

I am sure that a lot of hunters have done that, but for me, I am limited to where I can hunt. I spend my time on national forest land over on Pine Mountain. There is public land around Pound Lake that has many turkeys, but it is highly hunted—and that can make it more of a challenge. In areas where there is a plethora of hunters, one must be extremely careful. Some hunters forget about safety and do some crazy things to bag a turkey. More on that later.

The day after hunting season began, on April 15, I went fishing at Pound Lake. Since hunting isn't allowed on Sundays in Virginia, I wasn't worried about the dangers of careless hunters. About an hour before dark, I heard a turkey gobbling up on a ridge. I decided to be there before daylight the next day.

The next morning, I launched my boat and went up the lake near the ridge. After tying my boat to a tree, I began my ascent up the hill, moving as quietly as I could. I did not want to get too close.

At exactly daylight, the tom began gobbling from his roost about two hundred yards away. I commenced the routine I use to get a turkey's attention. First, I made what I call a "sleepy yelp," the sound a hen would make just before flying down from her roost. Then, I used my cap to make a flopping sound like a turkey would make flying down.

The tom answered with a double gobble, very interested in what he had just heard. I knew that there was a flock of hens nearby and that he would want to go to them.

I moved in closer, hoping to draw him in, but I heard him fly down and move off toward this flock.

At that moment, it became a game of cat and mouse. I began trying to anticipate which direction the hens would go and relocated to get into a good position for a shot at the tom.

After three or four movements, I heard a hen in the flock yelp, so I answered with my own yelp. She immediately left her flock and actually ran in my direction. The rest of her flock, along with the tom, began following.

She got about twenty yards from me and became suspicious. I was fully camouflaged—even with gloves on and was resting my back against a big oak tree. Apparently, I moved just enough for her to see me, and after a few seconds of limbo, she flew off.

I could see the flock about forty yards away. They would not come any closer and were gradually moving away from me. I decided to take a shot at the gobbler, but I missed, and he flew away. I checked the range and gauged the distance at forty-five yards. At that moment, I also decided to invest in a good rifle with an open sight.

I came off the hill to my boat, intending to return home. There was a light rain falling. I heard a gobbler sounding off about one-half mile away. He was really gobbling his head off, so what else could I do? I changed my plans. I retrieved my boat, motored up the lake and tied the boat up at the safest place and closest place to the tom. Way up on the top of the ridge, I heard a hen yelping. Now, it has been my practice to assume that any turkey call in the woods is not made by a turkey. Even a gobbling sound might be another hunter.

I set off for the top of the ridge. The gobbler was about one hundred yards on the other side of the ridge.

Upon reaching the top, I sat down against a big oak tree and made a soft purring sound, followed by a clucking sound. Immediately, there was a hen's yelp. I had two things on my mind at that time that, in retrospect, prevented a tragedy. First, I assumed the yelp was another hunter, so I knew I needed to be on guard. Second, I had previously decided to take only a head shot if a tom presented at close range. By now, it was raining hard. I saw movement in an ivy thicket and heard some twigs snap.

The first thing I saw was a hen moving in my direction. I then saw a gobbler's tail feathers—all fanned out—moving around as if in full strut. The turkeys were only about twenty yards away, and I was quite tempted to go ahead and shoot, but I had already committed myself to waiting for the head shot.

I began raising my gun to a shooting position. What happened next terrified me. Two hunters completely covered in camouflage crawled out of the ivy, carrying their decoys. I could not believe what had just transpired. These two were holding their decoys and moving them around just like a hen and a strutting tom.

I waved to them to let them know I was there. They noticed me and just stood there and stared. I left those two very lucky boys and made my way out of the woods. It was now pouring rain, and by the time I made it back to my boat and loaded it on the trailer, I was soaking wet.

I didn't go back into the woods again for over a week. The reality of what might have happened made me shudder every time I thought about it.

The following morning found me on Pine Mountain walking a four-wheeler trail. I discovered a couple of sandy places where turkeys had been wallowing. My plan was to amble along calling softly every now and then.

Without warning, I heard something walking toward me making quite a racket, so at first, I thought it was a deer. A hen came into view and I watched her begin jumping up and down under a little sourwood bush. I wondered what she was up to. She leaped up three or four times, then she left. I was curious as to what she had found, so I walked over for a closer look. I carefully examined the bush, but could not see anything of interest.

About six hours later, I found out what it was. After leaving the sourwood bush, I walked the trail for another hour or so, then began making my way back toward home. I was calling softly when a hen came in and a gobbler was following her. I was just standing there, out in the open, when she spotted me and flew off. The gobbler, about fifty yards away, was looking wondering what had spooked her. He began coming toward me. I shot him in the chest; this one did not fly away.

He was not a real trophy, but I was pleased with him. When I began dressing him out, I found that his crawl was full of green worms, sort of like a caterpillar but bright green. At once, I realized what the hen was after.

I got to thinking that these worms would make excellent bait for bluegills, so being the genius that I am on such matters, I returned to the site of the sourwood bush. I discovered that these worms were feeding on the leaves of these bushes. I collected a couple dozen of them and drove to Pound Lake. Just as I thought, the bluegills loved them and would nab them as soon as they hit water. Since it was nesting season for bluegills, I tried allowing a green worm to sink down to their nesting bed. They snatched them up faster than any bait I had ever tried.

I got to hunt a couple more times that season but had no more action. I thought long and hard about what might easily have happened to the two hunters I had encountered. Hunters must use common sense in the woods. Please do not carry decoys around. Certainly, do not hold onto them trying to attract a turkey. Such actions could only lead to tragedy. Also, never assume that a gobble or a yelp is actually a turkey.

Wearing blaze orange might lessen my chance of bagging a turkey, but from now on, that is exactly what I am going to do. Even just an orange cap might save a life.

Spring hunting for wild gobblers is an exciting and challenging sport; I was sad to see the season come to an end.

The Bear Who Was Afraid of a Turkey Decoy

When the sun came up on the morning of May 10, 2010, it found me sitting against a big pine tree listening for turkeys. I had gotten up early so that I could get set up before daylight. I had placed two blow-up decoys, a hen and a jake, about twenty yards away.

I heard a crashing sound off to my right. I turned my head in that direction and saw a huge black bear walking toward me.

My first thought was that he would catch my scent and go off in another direction. But the bear kept getting closer and closer. The course on which he was walking would put him right on top of me. A couple of times he lifted his head, sniffed the air and shook that big head.

I was armed with a 20-gauge shotgun loaded with #5 shot. The last thing I wanted to do was shoot him, which probably would cause him to run off and suffer great pain before dying.

My anxiety grew as the bear got closer and closer. When he was about ten yards away, I thought, "I am going to have to do something like stand up and yell."

About that time, he saw my decoys. He stopped and stared at them for two or three minutes. Then he started moving very slowly toward them.

He paused about ten feet away and glared, sniffing as if puzzled why these turkeys did not run or fly away. He moved around behind them, shifting from side to side, sniffing and stretching his head out toward them.

It actually became comical as this great bear, weighing over five hundred pounds, was seemingly afraid of those decoys. He again started inching toward them. He appeared to be ready to dash away if attacked by the decoys.

At long last, he reached them, and then did an amazing thing. He lowered his mouth over the jake's head. He did not bite down, just held the head in his mouth.

He stood that way for at least a minute. I feared that he would bite a hole in it.

"Hey! You leave my decoy alone!" I bellowed. He acted as if he never even heard me. I yelled again, waving my arms in the air. The bear raised his head and stared at me for a full minute. Uh-oh! He stared away, then he turned and studied me once again. He took one step forward, glanced my way a final time, and walked on off out of sight.

Is It Wrong to Hunt?

Is it wrong to kill wild animals? We are living in a day in which groups like PETA (People for the Ethical Treatment of Animals) are organizing to stop hunting and fishing. Some people have largely made up their minds on this subject, and I do not expect to change many minds by what I say here.

I absolutely agree that intentional mistreatment or negligence in the care of any creature is a major sin in the eyes of our God. When I see people with dogs or cats or farm animals with no shelter from the sun, rain, or other elements, when these creatures have nothing on which to sleep and not enough to eat, it really riles me. Anybody with any heart at all should be upset about this and report it to the proper authorities.

Allow me to share a couple of examples. When neighbors in a nearby apartment moved out, they left their dog tied up in the mud and rain with no bed and no food. My wife and I would take it something to eat, and once we even untied it and let it go free. Days later, the people returned to pick up more of their house wares and tied the dog back up. For three days we watched to see what they were going to do, but evidently they had abandoned it. I went to the chief of police and told him what had happened. He got very upset. He said that he was ready to prosecute the owners if they came back. I asked him if we could take the dog home; he was glad for us to do that. We later gave the dog to some folks who took very good care of it.

On another occasion, two young, helpless puppies were the victims. My son and I went down to do some crappie fishing. This was in January. The temperature was very cold—maybe in the teens. We had driven the boat a half-mile down the lake when we heard this wailing sound coming from a cove. We moved over to investigate and saw one of the saddest sights. Someone had apparently dropped off two puppies—out in the middle of nowhere, no chance for them to make it out, even to someone else's house. They were too little to travel far. One of the puppies was already dead and the other was curled up against the body of its dead companion. What a sad, lonely sight! We brought the live one home, but the next morning he, too, died.

I cannot express how disgusted and angry my son and I were at whoever did that. They had absolutely no mercy on these little dogs. What a twisted mind.

One time, I was delivering supplies to a mine in Phelps, Kentucky. A puppy was sitting on the side of the road. I stopped to see about him and heard a dog barking down below the road in the woods. I hiked down the hill to investigate and was amazed by what I found and how cruel people can be. A dog, probably the mother of the pup, was tied up in a burlap sack and left to starve and die an absolutely miserable death.

I hurriedly cut the sack open. She immediately took off running farther down the hill, apparently looking for water. I took the pup home, and my dad took him in.

I feel that there is no excuse for this. There are animal shelters readily available, and adoption is commonplace.

God has words to say about our responsibility to our animals. Psalm 50:10 and 11 say, "For every beast of the forest is Mine, the cattle on a thousand hills. I know every bird of the mountains, and everything that moves in the field is Mine." Another verse that says it very succinctly is Proverbs 12:10: "A righteous man has regard for the life of his animal, but even the compassion of the wicked is cruel." I would not want to be in their shoes someday when God makes these kinds of things right.

We hunters and fishermen need to lead the way in taking care of the animals in our world—tame or wild. Never cause suffering.

Rabbits in the Snow

We had a "rabbit snow" a few days ago. Upon looking out our window, I saw the tracks of a rabbit in my wife's flowerbed. I could already smell the rich aroma of cooking meat and taste the gravy made from the broth. Thick socks were pulled out of the drawer and put on, coveralls were next, followed by boots. I added a toboggan cap and grabbed my gun.

The rabbit's tracks came down the hill, into the flowerbed, and through some trees. I began to see tracks going into brush piles and out, into briar patches and out—tracks were all over! I have found that rabbits like to hide in these piles and patches, under an old fallen tree, or better yet, in a hole in the ground. Most of the time, though, they will be just sitting somewhere outside.

Just below our house is a heap of tree stumps uprooted when we had our land excavated. Every time it snows, I check, and sure enough, tracks are there where the rabbit came out to feed and then retreated to the safety of the pile. In the past, I have kicked the pile, beat on it with a log, and poked sticks into it, but the rabbit always refuses to come out.

When you are tracking a rabbit, you have to be ready, watching very carefully for him to dart away. You need to know where he *might* go. When his tracks lead toward, say, a brush pile, I like to cautiously circle it to see if there are any tracks leading out. Obviously, if the tracks are going in and not coming out, you would have him pinpointed. Sometimes, you think you have him cornered only to find out, somehow, he is not there. Rabbits are very smart!

If you are hunting by yourself, you have to move slowly, kicking at brush and stomping the ground. When Mr. Rabbit makes his exit, he is going to be moving quite quickly. He will dodge trees, run under logs, and do everything "animally" possible to avoid capture. He knows he is a favorite prey.

If you have rabbit dogs, it is probably best to leave them home as they will mess up the tracks. You might consider keeping one handy to let loose only if the rabbit gets away.

On this particular snowy day, I tracked my rabbit to a forgotten and rusted drainpipe. There were tracks going in but none coming out. All I had to do was kick the pipe and away he ran. I missed with the first shot but got him with the second. (I use a 20-gauge double-barrel shotgun with #7 shot in one barrel and #4 or #5 in the other. The latter has more range.)

Some of my best memories growing up were of the days we brought in a good mess of rabbits for both my uncle's family and mine. Rabbit meat is different from any other meat. It is rated as one of the highest in protein among wild game. My mom would cook the meat overnight in a crock pot and then roll it in flour and fry it. She would then make gravy, using cream mixed with the rabbit broth. I fix mine this way, too.

Hunting rabbits in the snow can get in your blood. Look for them on old mining strip jobs or in forgotten apple orchards. Rabbits seem to favor the roughest brush possible. Be sure to wear your blaze orange cap and/or vest. If you are hunting with a partner or two, know where your buddies are at all times. You may just be disappointed when February comes and the season is over.

Striper Fishing, June 1996

Have you ever gone on a fishing trip and have no action until near the end of the trip and you find yourself catching fish one after the other? My wife and I had such an experience on Cherokee Lake. School had let out for the summer, and my eight-year-old son had gone to stay with his aunt for a few days.

I suggested to my wife that we go down to German Creek Boat Dock and rent a cabin. We hitched our boat onto the back of our truck, loaded our fishing gear, and headed out. I had stayed in a cabin on German Creek many years before and was looking forward to staying there again. On my last trip there, with my brother, we were put in Cabin #4. To me, it was a nice cabin with board walls, two beds, electric stove, refrigerator, and air conditioner.

We pulled up and stopped in front of the office and went in. To my disappointment, they told me that #4 had burned down a while before, but they had other cabins available, so I paid for one night. We pulled up in front of the cabin and went inside.

What we found were cockroaches running around and an air conditioner that wouldn't work. My wife was totally disgusted and was ready to go back home.

I went back to the office and told them about our problems. They found us a nicer, cleaner cabin where the air conditioner worked. My wife got out a can of Lysol disinfectant spray and sprayed down the entire cabin before she would allow our stuff to be brought in. My wife adds here that she cried the whole time when preparing steaks on the tiny range. She states, too, that if this cabin had been ours, even with its ragged furnishings, as long as it was cleaned (by her), it would have been like home.

We rested up for a couple hours and went on the lake to fish. We fished hard until well after dark. I caught one bass, and that was all the action we had for that day.

The next morning, we decided to do some trolling. We trolled steadily for a couple hours without even getting a bite. Checkout time was eleven o'clock, so we packed up to go home. As we were driving, I suggested that we try fishing once again. There is a public launch ramp not far from Cherokee Boat Dock, so we put in there. We went up to about the 26-mile marker. Bass were breaking up in a cove, and we fished for a while but could not get the fish to bite.

Some rain clouds were moving in, so we decided to head in before the rain began. On the way, we happened upon a big school of shad. I threw out my net and encircled a throng of them. We picked out about four dozen and put them in the livewell. Shad minnows cause the water in a livewell to foam up, which kills them. I had brought along a bottle of Foam Out, which I poured in the water along with some Shad Alive powder.

We motored down Poor Valley and tied up under the 25E bridge and had not been there long before the rain came down in buckets. Fortunately, we were under the bridge.

I had a paper graph fish finder, and it showed some big fish directly under the boat. I grabbed a heavy rod and reel for my wife, loaded with fourteen-pound test, showed her how to put a shad on, and she dropped it down right beside the boat. Not even five seconds later, a striper snared her bait and began running hard. She had never caught a striper before. I never heard such squealing and hollering as the striper kept pulling the drag. "What do I do? What do I do?" she screamed.

Well, there was not much that could be done as the striper had wrapped around the other side of the pylon we were tied to. Her rod was bent around the end of the post—all she could do was hang on. The run soon ended when the line snapped.

After we had rebaited the line, I instructed her to keep the striper from getting around the pylon. She threw her bait out, and the same thing happened again. A striper hit her shad almost instantly. The striper could not be stopped from wrapping the line around the concrete pylon. It, too, snapped the line.

Now the only thing I could do was to demonstrate the correct technique for hooking and pulling in a big striper. The same thing happened to me, as I could not stop the striper and he broke off.

We took time to switch to heavier line – 17 lb. Trilene XT. The heavier line enabled us to stop them before they got the line wrapped around the concrete pylons. The tougher line held even when it was frayed.

We saw a storm was coming and were glad to be tied up under the bridge. When the rain came, we were high and dry, catching and releasing one stripper after another. My wife caught and then released a huge largemouth bass. This trip tops my list of favorite fishing trips!

The Legend of Falling Rocks

As you drive along mountain roads, occasionally you see a sign that says, "WATCH FOR FALLING ROCKS." I always assumed, and I guess everyone else did, too, that there may be rocks in the road that had rolled off the hillside. Now, it is always good to watch for rocks in the road, because to hit one may damage your car. I am writing this story to set the record straight on what the sign actually means.

Long ago, there was an Indian village called Cherokeearapaho. The chief of this village had two sons: one was named "Falling Rocks," the other, "Butterfly." The Indians had a unique way of naming their sons and daughters. When the baby was born, the daddy Indian would look out the tepee door, and the first thing he saw became the infant's name. For example, he might see a three-legged dog and name his child "Three-Legged Dog." Or he might see a skunk chasing a stupid chicken and would name the child "Stinking Skunk Chasing Stupid Chicken."

I can imagine the Indian chiefs, sitting around the fire in a pow-wow, deciding whether to start a war against the Winnebago. The Big Chief would ask each young but upcoming chief to give his opinion.

Big Chief: "What say, Stinking Skunk Chasing Stupid Chicken?"

With a name like that, he probably would not get much respect.

(We need to interject here what this war council was all about. The Cherokeearapaho thought they had been cheated. The Cherokeearapaho raised chickens. The Winnebago raised pigs. There was a deal in which the Cherokeearapaho would trade the Winnebago 6,000 chickens for 3,013 pigs. When the Winnebago delivered the pigs, there were only thirteen pigs, three of them sows. The Cherokeearapaho thought they were going to receive 3,013 pigs. The problem was that the Winabagos had agreed to three sows and thirteen pigs. Just a misunderstanding, but enough to start a war.)

What if the baby was a girl? Dad looks out the tepee door and sees a snake swallowing a baby rabbit.

Big Chief: "Her name is 'Bunny Being Swallowed By Snake.'"

I imagine Mommy Indian would gently suggest that Dad keep looking. If Dad refused, she would not so gently use what was then called a "veto stick." Today, we call them "rolling pins."

I have heard (I do not know if it is true) that other cultures had unique ways of naming babies. For instance, when a baby was born, dad would maybe throw some pots and pans against the wall. The sound (or the racket) was what they named the child. Names such as "Cling Clong Tinkle Pop" were not uncommon. Maybe Dad decides to use only an iron skillet to simplify things. The pan would hit the wall with a *clong* and hit the ground with a *clunk*, so the baby was named "Clong Clunk." Clong Clunk may be all right for a boy, but not so appropriate for a girl. I am sure this culture's mom used her type of veto stick to convince dad to keep throwing.

Back to Falling Rocks and Butterfly. Falling Rocks got his name when dad looked outside and saw some rocks falling over. I have no idea what caused the rocks to fall over; the legend does not say.

You might assume that Butterfly got his name because Dad saw a butterfly lighting on a flower. Not so. According to legend, a woman needed some butter, so she stepped out the door of her tepee and yelled, "Can I borrow a stick of butter?" to the woman in the tepee next door. The next-door neighbor was kind enough to throw a stick of butter out to her. The dad saw the butter flying through the air and named his boy "Flying Butter." As time went on, his name morphed into "Butterfly."

Many, many moons later, the boys were grown up. Dad was growing old and one of the boys would soon take his place as chief. Dad called the boys together and explained how one would be chosen to be the new chief.

The boys were to go out on a hunt to bring back a trophy animal. Butterfly came back dragging a 3,000-pound grizzly bear, all trussed up and still alive.

Falling Rocks heard what his brother had brought in. He left camp and began hunting. According to the legend, he is still looking for an animal that will surpass his brother's catch. So, that is what the road signs really mean: everyone keep their eyes open and "Watch for Falling Rocks."

Tunnel Catfish with Allen and Jimmy Graham

June 1988, John Sevier Steam Plant

A friend of mine, Claude, now deceased, and his son, Allen, had been telling me about something they had discovered down at the John Sevier Steam Plant. They were catching very large flathead catfish.

Now, for a little background. Most of my experience at the steam plant was fishing for white bass during the spring spawning run. I had had good fishing, usually with my brothers and some of our friends. Also, in the spring, the smallmouth bass moved in and occasionally we caught some really nice ones. You could catch drum, huge carp, channel catfish—seemed like every fish in the lake moved up to the steam plant March through June.

Claude had told me about tunnels through which water from the Holsten River was piped up into the steam plant for cooling down its furnaces, and about the outlet tunnels where the used water would gush out. This was prime fishing water. I was invited by Allen and Claude's brother, Jimmy, to go fishing with them on a Friday night. On the way down, they were excitedly telling me stories of the big fish they had caught, which made me anxious to get there and experience it for myself. We arrived at the parking lot and gathered our gear and began walking over to the river. It was a very cold night for June, and I was glad I had brought along a coat.

It was about a half-mile walk and, as usual on a weekend night, there were a lot of other fishermen. Allen said he hoped that there would be a spot where we could fish, with no one there. We came around the trail, and Allen announced that the place we wanted was vacant, so we got to a calm spot in the normally boiling water. The water was very dingy, so we could not see at all what was in there, even though it was only four feet deep. Allen showed how they had learned to catch those big flatheads of the tunnels. He explained that the water was moving up inside the tunnels and the trick was to find the opening and allow the current to carry the bait back up inside the tunnel. There was only enough space for two lines at one tunnel, so I just watched to see how they did it. Allen would drop the night crawler down and use the end of the rod to find the tunnel opening, then give slack in the line to allow the bait to be carried up inside the tunnel. The bait actually was back behind us, up under the hillside that covered the tunnel. After about fifteen minutes, Allen's rod started jerking and was about to be pulled into the water. He grabbed his pole and set the hook on something very big. The problem was getting the catfish out of the tunnel into open water without getting the line frayed and breaking. The openings of the tunnels were constructed of concrete and could, therefore, easily fray the line. The trick was to stick the rod down into the water and try to just wench the fish out of the tunnel, keeping the line away from the tunnel opening. If you held the rod up out of the water, the catfish would usually break off. Jimmy had fifty-pound test line break when he tried to stand up and drag it out without putting his rod in the water. Allen knew what to do from experience and he soon had the big fish out of the tunnel, out into the channel, where the water was very swift. Using heavy line, he was able to wear the fish down and land it. It was a huge flathead. I could put both of my fists in its mouth. About one half hour later, Allen hooked another big fish and again dragged it out of the tunnel into the swift water, where the tussle really began. After about fifteen minutes, the catfish wore down enough to drag it upon the bank. It was another flathead bigger than the first one.

Later on, Allen told me to try it and turned the tunnel over to me. It was difficult to get the bait up inside the tunnel, but I finally did. I did not get a bite for about two hours, then my line started moving back up inside the tunnel. My rod tip was jerking, indicating I had one on. After about ten minutes, I landed a channel catfish weighing about ten pounds. Fishing was very slow that night. I only got one more bite and hooked a big, heavy fish and while trying to maneuver him out of the tunnel, he pulled loose.

The combined weight of our three fish was over one hundred

pounds. We had brought a couple of grass potato sacks to bring our fish back home. We soaked the sacks in water, but only needed one to carry our fish. We got a pole and tied the sack on it and carried it between two of us. People were amazed by our transportation method and the fish flopping around inside the sack.

We loaded our gear and fish back into the truck and started for home, about a two-hour drive. The sack came open and the fish slid out into the bed of the truck. All the way home, those big catfish slid back and forth on their bellies and they were still living when we got home. We took them to a big pond and set them free and they swam off.

Fishing with Roger – A Tribute

Roger was the best fisherman I have ever fished with. I never went on a trip with him that we didn't catch fish.

I remember a trip we made to Smith Mountain Lake near Roanoke, Virginia. Neither of us had ever been on that lake, so we didn't know what to expect.

We fished in an aluminum boat that we had rented from the boat dock. We had our own gas and electric motors. The first day, we fished hard, trying every kind of lure in our tackle boxes, without getting one bite.

About an hour before dark, we moved up on a bank that looked good, with brush piles and logs in the water. Up until then, we had used only artificial bait. We had brought a bunch of night crawlers to use after dark for catfish. Roger put a night crawler on his hook and threw out close to the shoreline and let it sink naturally.

I figured that we would only catch bluegills using night crawlers, but about thirty seconds later, I was proven wrong when his line straightened out and went sideways. Roger set the hook, and I watched as a nice largemouth jumped into the air, shaking his head trying to remove the hook.

I was throwing a crankbait, not convinced that this fish was not just a fluke. A minute later, I was proven wrong again when he landed another nice largemouth.

I took my crankbait off and tied on a hook. I strung the head of the night crawler, like Roger was doing, and threw out close to the bank. Immediately my line started moving fast, and I set the hook on a fifteen-inch bass. We fished until dark, landing one bass after another. I believe that we caught and released twenty bass before dark.

That night, we fished a couple hours for catfish and caught about four or five. The thing I remember most was how hard the fish could pull. They were not exceptionally big, the largest being about twenty inches long, but these catfish pulled harder than any catfish I had ever caught. I also remember getting stung by one, and it gave me a really bad headache. Fortunately, Roger had some Goody's Powder, which gave me relief.

The next day, we went back to the bank where we had fished the day before. We were out of night crawlers, so we went back to artificial lures and we caught several more bass. The trick was to throw the lures right to the edge of the bank and reel it close to some kind of structure. The bass would hit as the lure went by. In all, we caught thirty to forty bass.

Roger and I also took a fishing trip to South Holston Lake and fished for crappie. I had installed a Lowrance Mach I Fish Finder on my boat. It was the kind of fish finder that used rolls of special paper. I was anxious to try it out, hoping we could find schools of crappie headed up the lake. We saw a lot of fishermen out. A boat was tied up at every brush pile, logjam, and fallen tree.

Roger said we should look for stained water around the mouth of coves or points. We pulled up at the mouth of a cove that had brush piles and fallen trees all up in the cove. There were two or three boats tied up to one of these structures, and they didn't seem to be catching any fish.

My first cast, using a Roadrunner, was hit by a nice crappie. We began to catch one crappie after another for a couple hours, then moved the boat, looking for another spot with stained water. Again, it was one fish after another. We must have caught over a hundred fish that day! Roger was right on when he said fish would not be around structures, but on points with stained water.

Roger told me about a striper-fishing trip he took to Boone Lake. He said that he was cruising up the Watauga fork of the lake, looking for breading fish, when he came upon a school of breaking stripers. He cast out a bucktail jig and hooked a big striper. He said the striper pulled so hard, he had to follow it with his boat. The next thing he knew, he was right in the middle of the school of stripers. He said there were so many fish, it looked like he could step out of his boat and walk on their backs. The fish Roger caught that trip averaged twenty pounds, with the largest weighing forty-three pounds.

At the time I am writing this, Roger has brain cancer. I have gone to visit him a few times, and we talked about our experiences on the land and water. The cancer is spreading fast, and we are told that he only has a short time to live. I know I will miss him and the fun times we had just talking about the great outdoors. He was very cheerful and expects to wake up in Heaven, where his mom and dad are waiting.

From the Past: Hunting the Ruffed Grouse

Thump, Thump, Thump, Thump, Thump, Thump, Thump, Thump, Thump, Thump, Thump, Thump, Thump, Thump. This is the sound of a ruffed grouse drumming his wings in the spring and fall. He starts out with four Thumps about two seconds apart, then gets faster and faster, ending with two slow Thumps. He can be heard about one-half mile away. The drumming lasts about ten to twelve seconds. Growing up in the woods, I have heard this sound many times. Sadly, this sound is seldom heard anymore. According to the *National Audubon Society Field Guide to North American Birds*, the suitable habitat is disappearing. In many areas, forests are maturing, eliminating the undergrowth this species needs. Wild turkeys are increasing and the grouse are decreasing.

Grouse have amazing eyesight and hearing. Believe it or not, on three separate occasions, I was in my treestand watching for deer when a grouse flew in and landed about twenty yards away. Somehow the grouse detected me, even though I did not move or make a sound. The grouse walked slowly toward a small tree limb that had fallen. It went under it and that was the last I saw of it. When I came down from my stand, it was gone. Although I had been watching carefully, I never did see the grouse again. How he managed to sneak off without me seeing was amazing. It had to walk right through open ground without being seen or heard.

Trying to sneak up on a grouse that is drumming is nearly impossible. My dad told how he had figured out a way to do it. When he had located a drumming grouse, he would walk up near where he was drumming. Grouse would always use an old fallen tree so he could watch out for predators. My dad would start scratching the leaves away going backwards away from where he had been. The grouse had flown off on his way in, but dad knew he would eventually return to the log.

Dad would clear out a trail for about two hundred yards. He would go home and wait for the grouse to return, usually in a day or two.

Dad would very quietly make his way to the end of the path he had made and wait for the grouse to start drumming. When the grouse had beaten his wings four times, he would move toward him. Dad said the grouse closes his eyes during the fast drumming parts. Dad would try to make it to an object like a tree or bush to hide behind or go down on his knees. The trick was to stop and remain still, not moving again until the grouse started drumming again. Dad would repeat this process over and over, getting closer every time he drummed.

Sometimes there would be only three to five minutes between drummings, and at other times, up to one-half hour.

The object was to get to the end of the trail without being detected by the grouse. If dad was fortunate enough to make it within range, he could get a shot off. He said his success rate was about fifty percent. Hunting grouse is not only a great sporting experience; they also make very tasty table fare.

From the Past: Renegade Bear

My grandmother, Fronia Greene, would often tell us this story when my brother and I would stay the night with her.

My grandmother was born in 1890. Her grandmother lived in the early to mid 1800s, somewhere in Virginia or Kentucky. In those days, there were numerous animals such as buffalo, elk, deer, and black bear. Her grandmother—my great-great-grandmother—lived in a cabin somewhere around the Ramsey section of Norton, Virginia. She kept her children under constant watch because of the threat from Indians. They were known to capture people and take them far away to their villages. Often, those loved ones were never seen or heard from again.

Another threat was from panthers. These big cats would scream at night right outside their cabin.

The people in those days mostly raised their own food. They had pigs, cows, goats, sheep, and bees. The beehives were built with heavy and thick wood, hopefully making them bear proof.

One night my great-great-grandmother and her family were sitting around their fireplace when they heard the sound of wood cracking and splintering. The dogs started going wild and got as close to the family's cabin as possible. They knew what was about.

The man of the house, my great-great-grandfather, stepped out with a lantern and a double-barrel shotgun. He got a glimpse of a huge animal running away, and he shot both barrels at it, then ran back into the cabin and bolted the door.

At dawn, they all went out to investigate and found one of their beehives totally ripped apart. Bolted to stout 4x4s were solid oak boards, an inch thick, and these were shredded. Some of the 4x4s were damaged beyond reuse. Nearby were huge bear tracks. The awesome power of the bear made their hair stand up on the backs of their necks.

The beehive was irreparable. The hive was lost. The family knew that the bear would return, so they set about making the remaining beehives as secure as possible. They added more strong boards to the hives and built a fence around them.

My great-great-grandfather stayed up that night with his rifle, in case the bear returned. Losing a beehive could be not be tolerated, so the bear had to be stopped.

Nothing happened that night or the next night. Grandfather decided to give up his vigil, hoping that the bear would not return. The next morning, though, they checked on their hives, and what they saw was a disaster. The bear had smashed through the fence as if it were not there and destroyed another beehive. It is unclear why the family did not hear this. (A friend of mine had a beehive, the frame of which was made of solid steel. One night, a bear ripped the hive apart. He said pieces of the hive were scattered all over.)

I discussed the story of the bear and the beehive with a biologist from the Department of Game and Inland Fisheries. He stated that a big boar bear can lose all fear of man, especially if it has not had a bad experience or been injured. I know this from my experience with a huge bear I encountered while turkey hunting (described in my story, "The Bear That Was Afraid of a Turkey Decoy"). That big boar knew where I was sitting and kept walking closer and closer to where I was. He did not alter his course for me.

Back to the renegade bear. A man with a pack of bear hounds went out after the boar. His hounds caught the scent and tracked him. This was quite easy because the boar chose not to run. A dozen hounds closed in on the bear, trying to keep him at bay. The bear rushed in among the pack of dogs, swinging his huge paws and killing dogs right and left. Before the hunter could catch up, only four dogs were left and two of these were wounded so badly they had to be put down. The big boar had disappeared.

My grandmother told how the bear became a total nuisance. He learned that cows, sheep, pigs, and horses were easy game and would smash down a fence and kill just for the fun of it. He could kill a horse with one blow from his big paw.

During those days, people depended on their livestock for food, plowing their gardens, and pulling logs for building and firewood. Men kept their guns at hand when they were out working or walking somewhere. Somehow, this bear had to be killed. They tried baiting the bear. Men hid in trees or in the lofts of their barns, but not one was able to draw a bead on the big boar. He could not be lured in. Someone did catch a fleeting glimpse of the bear and reported that he had a prominent white spot on his chest.

That same bear was later seen by a man and his wife on their little farm. Just before the Civil War, about 1850, over in Ramsey, Virginia, this couple lived alone in their cabin, and every day, he carried his gun with him as he worked around his farm. He left another gun at home for his wife. He had taught her how to pour in powder and shot and then add powder on the flash pan to fire the gun. One morning, she was home alone, hard at work on her chores. She had washed some clothes and picked up her laundry basket to hang the clothes outside to dry. When she opened the door, there sat a huge bear with a white spot on its chest, a mere thirty yards away, just staring at the cabin. She slammed the door shut and locked it. She quickly thought about what she should do, all the while hoping the bear would go away. She had some type of horn that she could blow (possibly an elk horn), which would signal her husband that he was needed at home. She picked up the horn, then put it back down, realizing that her husband would surely encounter the bear and might be injured or killed. Also, it was almost dinnertime, and before long, her husband would be coming home to eat.

She knew what she had to do, but felt she could not do it. She peeked outside and the bear was still there, watching the cabin.

She had never fired the gun before and had never loaded it herself, only watched her husband as he demonstrated the process. She began to recall the steps he had explained. First, pour in a measure of powder. She couldn't remember how much powder to pour in, but she picked up the gun and poured in a decent amount. She thought, what if that wasn't enough? Too little powder might just wound the bear and make him furious. So she poured in some more, hesitated, and then added more. She didn't know it, but there was over three times more powder in the barrel than was necessary. She pushed a 60-caliber ball down in the barrel and checked the flint and the flashpan. Everything was ready for her to shoot, but still she was scared to fire the gun, worried what the bear might do if she missed.

She finally gritted her teeth and moved over to the door. She opened it just enough to stick the gun barrel out the crack. She took aim at the white spot on the bear's chest and pulled the trigger.

Her husband working in the field heard the explosion, loud as a cannon. It echoed for miles around the farm. He ran home to see what had happened.

Meanwhile, his wife was sprawled on the other side of the room with the gun lying near her. Obviously, there was a tremendous kick for which she was not prepared. The look on her face told it all. Imagine what the blast would do to one's hearing—coming from *inside* the cabin. The resulting smoke was too thick to see through.

Her husband found the massive boar lying on his back dead. There was a gaping hole right in the center of the white spot. The blast had been so powerful, it had instantly knocked the bear onto his back. He never moved.

The husband gathered his wife into his arms and hugged her proudly. He promised that he would show her the correct amount of powder to add. Who knows? Perhaps the triple amount of powder was what it took to take out the big boar.

Word got out and folks came from miles away to see the big bear and see for themselves that the great threat had been eliminated.

From the Past: A Sad Bear Story

My uncle Lloyd told this story about a mama bear and her two cubs. Mama bear climbed a large chestnut tree and her cubs followed her up. The cubs began playing. One of them got too rowdy, and as the practice of mama bears is, she spanked it by swatting it with her paw. The cub lost its grip and fell from the tree to the ground below. Mama hurried down, and found her baby. She called to it, but it did not move. She bawled and bawled, while pawing it gently. The little cub was dead. After a time, she and her lone cub walked away.

Carps

No book of hunting and fishing stories would be complete without a carp story. Dad took us boys—Jeff, Ronnie, and me—on many a trip camping out on Cherokee Lake in Tennessee. We would build a fire, put out some lanterns and fish for carp and catfish. Mostly, we caught carps. Carps can pull as hard as any other fish. They can sure stretch your line.

One trip, we were camped out at the lake's twenty-six-mile marker, fishing off a cliff into very deep water. Nothing was biting, so we started rolling big rocks off into the water to see how big a splash we could make.

Not long afterward, we started catching fish—carps. We must have caught two hundred pounds of fish that day! A ten-pounder was scoffed at as a little one. Two of the carps were too big to fit into our fishing net. Tip: Don't try this on a lake that has carps in it unless you really want to catch them.

On other fishing trips, we used to sneak up on carps that were "shoaling" or splashing around up close to the bank. They did this in the spring, usually during the month of May.

When you snag a carp close to his tail, as we tried to do, you had better be ready for a tremendous fight. They can pull twice as hard when hooked at the tail end.

Here is a true carp story you may not believe. When we lived in Kentucky, there was a creek that ran behind our house that had carps in it. I was, at the time, transitioning from job to job, so I had a few days off. In our creek, there was one carp that was larger than the others. My goal was to catch him, but it proved hard to get him to bite, much less to land him.

One cold and snowy morning, on a whim, I took a small rod and reel with four-pound test line and put on a #14 hook and a kernel of corn. I sneaked over to the creek and located the carp. I pitched the kernel of corn and let it settle in front of him. Immediately, he sucked it in, and I pulled lightly so as not to break the line. The fight was on!

This big boy fought around and around in the pool of water he was used to. Suddenly, he headed upstream. He lunged for a brush pile and got tangled up. Now, I had just taken a shower, and my hair was still wet, but even so I made up my mind to go after him. I jumped in (the water was freezing cold) and waded up to the brush pile. I managed to get him untangled by pulling away some branches and freeing up the line, and he swam back down the creek into deeper water, where he tangled the line again. I waded after him with the water up to my waist. Again, I succeeded in setting him free, but he headed back upstream with me splashing along behind him.

For twenty minutes, I chased him up and down the creek. The big carp finally managed to get back inside the roots of a large buckeye tree. I reached as far as I could under the tree to get ahold of him. I grasped him by the mouth and gills and brought him out to show my wife my trophy. She was not too impressed with the fish and thought I was crazy for wading in the creek in the freezing water.

This was on Saturday, March 4. On the 7th, I began to feel feverish and came down with a bad sore throat. The infection moved up into my ears and blood ran out of my ear. I woke up one night with everything spinning around and around. The next morning, I went to the emergency room and had to get a shot and some antibiotics. A week later, I was no better so I went to an ENT doctor. He gave me a shot and a big bottle of penicillin capsules. After my fishing adventure and the resulting sickness, I left the carps in our creek alone. They could be almost as dangerous as rabbits.

Chicken

I vaguely remember a time long ago when someone decided to give my family some chickens. The only problem was we had to catch them, as they were free-range chickens. We quickly found out that catching them was easier at night when they were on the roost. After capturing all the chickens, they became a source of entertainment, especially for me, being only about seven years old. My older sister claims that one of these became a pet chicken that would ride on my shoulder or the handlebars of my tricycle. She said that when I called it, it would come running. The chicken had a name, Black Gold. She thinks that is so funny and still enjoys telling people about it.

There was a creek that meandered by our house, through the woods. A few times, I had walked up and down that creek with my older brother and cousin and as long as I was with them, I was not afraid of anything. There was a big pool about half a mile down the creek that had a lot of fish in it. Some big ones were over four inches long! I longed to go to that pool and spend some time using my stick, my piece of sewing thread, and my bent stickpin, catching these monsters. My only fear was the many wild animals and Indians that were lurking behind every tree and rock along the way to the pool.

One day, I picked up my fishing gear, and with Black Gold riding on my shoulder, I had the nerve (barely!) to venture to the pool. On the way down, I was scared of every sound and each stump looked like a bear (no bears inhabited our area). At one point, a squirrel crossed the creek in front of us. It scared me, but Black Gold clucked at it a few times and the squirrel scampered off. Whew! It probably didn't depart due to my chicken's clucking, but in my little mind, Black Gold had run the intruder off. With my courage greatly increased, I continued on to the pool without another incident.

The water in the pool was clear enough to see the spectacular variety of hornyhead and silver sides that lurked in the depths (two feet) of the pool. I really do not remember if I caught anything, but I do remember that as I fished, I forgot all about the dangers around me. After all, Black Gold was near. After a couple hours, I began to worry again, and he and I decided we better go back home.

Huntin' Stupid Deer

Note: The person relating this story wishes to remain anonymous.

Patrick McManus, a humor writer for *Outdoor Life* (now retired), wrote stories that portrayed him as being too dumb and unlucky to outsmart an animal or fish. He also somehow managed to jinx other sportsmen who hunted and fished with him. In his book, *The Night the Bear Ate Goombaw* (1989), there is a story entitled "The Dumbest Antelope." The only possible way McManus could kill an antelope was to find one that was quite dumb. He would have to get close enough—about 25 yards—to make the shot. His hunting party spent a lot of their time out in the field looking for such an animal.

This is a story about a deer that was very stupid; he was asking to be shot.

This hunter I know spent every day in the woods during the 1977 deer season. Other hunters managed to bag a deer. The last day of the season rolled around, and this hunter had not gotten even one glimpse of a deer. At this point, I'm going to stop to give this hunter a name, making it easier for me to write about him. "R3D3" will be his assigned name.

Saturday morning, the last day of the season, was very, very cold with six inches of new snow and a terrible wind. R3D3 had no intention of going back up on the top of High Knob, as it was too cold and windy for any self-respecting deer to be out and about.

Some other hunters talked R3D3 into going, because they said only very stupid deer would be tracking around in weather that bad. They also had a four-wheel drive truck.

So, four brave hunters crammed into the cab of the pickup, heading out of forty degrees below to where it was really cold.

Well, did he find a really stupid deer, you ask?

After going their separate ways, R3D3 started down an old logging road. He saw where a really stupid deer had walked down to a patch of laurel with a creek running through it. That deer was standing in the creek. Of all places to hide, he picked a creek. Not in a sunny spot. Not in a sheltered cove. In a creek.

All at once, the stupid deer lost his bravado and took off. R3D3 brought his gun up and fired in the general direction the deer was going.

The deer had almost shifted into high gear when the 150 grain 7mm Remington Magnum bullet caught up to the back of his head, knocking the deer end over end at least five times.

That had to be one of the luckiest shots I had ever made. That poor deer, it just was not his day.

Living in Safer Times

My family and I lived in the mountains of Southwest Virginia. We resided in a cinderblock house that my dad built before I was born. Unlike pioneers of long ago, we never had to worry about Indians, bears, mountain lions, or any other really dangerous creatures.

I grew up with three brothers and one sister. Until we got an electric range installed about 1968, we had to gather wood to heat the old Warm Morning cook stove. Mom used to get up and start a fire in the firebox to heat up the stove. She usually made biscuits and gravy each morning. She would put the biscuits in the oven, which took them what seemed forever to get done. The stove door had a built-in thermometer, and when the needle reached a certain point—about 350 degrees—the biscuits would be done. Many a time we would sit in the kitchen and watch the needle move so slowly. It took well over an hour for the biscuits to get done. Along with the usual gravy and biscuits, we would have fried eggs and bacon. We raised our own chickens and hogs, where we got eggs, bacon, pork chops and steaks. Every now and then, Mom would pick out a chicken to have for supper. We used to enjoy chasing down the one she wanted. Mom was very good at the chopping block.

The school I went to was a big two-room wooden structure. It had three grades in each room—grades 1-3 and grades 4-6. During recess, we would have make-believe games, usually cowboys and Indians. One of our favorite games—spurred on by Mr. Riner, the 4th-6th grade teacher—was to chase the girls, and when we caught them, we would put them in the well house. The girls were none too happy about this; I never have understood why.

In the wintertime, we would ride our sleds on the nearby public road, making it slicker and slicker for any traffic trying to get into town.

Another fun activity was to find a grapevine that was firmly fastened up in the top branches of a large tree. We would cut the vine at the base and then back it up the hill as far as the grapevine would reach, get a good grip, and cast ourselves off. Some grapevines would not get very high but still gave a good ride—as far as 100 feet long. One particular grapevine was cut on the side of a steep hill. It was the favorite of my brothers, our neighborhood boys, and me. Seeing that it was on such a steep hill, this vine would allow you to swing fifty feet off the ground. There was a big tree limb high up in a nearby oak tree. This grapevine would hit that limb, and of course, the vine would stop—that is, all except the bottom ten feet or so. The momentum found us parallel to the ground. You talk about dangerous—this was.

"You'll shoot your eye out." That's what the teacher and Santa Claus and mom all told the kid in the movie, *Christmas Story*. This little guy had made known that all he really wanted for Christmas was a BB gun. My neighbors, Danny and Cody, and myself used to engage in BB wars with my older brother, Ronnie. It was us three little guys against Ronnie, who was three or four years older than we were. We little guys built a rock wall about one hundred yards away from Ronnie—he had assured us he had no use for anything to hide behind. Ronnie would dart around, firing at us with his gun. Our rock wall served its purpose, keeping us from getting hit. Ronnie, who didn't have both oars in the water, got hit a lot. See how really safe we were?

I remember reading a journal by Christopher Gist who spent a lot of time exploring the mountains of Southwest Virginia and Southeast Kentucky somewhere in the early 1700s. He wrote about all the big game animals he saw. I don't remember the exact numbers, but he saw large elk herds, buffalo, bears, and lots of deer and turkeys.

When I was growing up, the only animals around for us to hunt were small game, like rabbits, squirrels, grouse, and groundhogs. Groundhogs were especially a nuisance to people's gardens. I used to get calls from people, especially older folks, asking me to come to try to eliminate some of these hogs. One older lady, whose older son still lived with her, called on me several times. I would show up with my .22, and we would sit on the front porch and watch. I very seldom saw a groundhog. It's like they knew I was watching for them. Their holes were all over, showing that they were there, but when I was around they stayed put. In all the times we sat on the front porch, I only killed one groundhog.

In the early days, settlers had to worry about raiding Indian parties, panthers, bears, and all kinds of poisonous snakes. As you can see from our growing-up days, we lived without much danger, as we did not have to worry about those things our forefathers had to deal with.

Snakes were very plentiful, however. They used to inhabit our playgrounds, which were just about everywhere we could walk through in a day. Copperheads were in abundance. I remember my dad telling us a story several times about a copperhead that was attacking folks when they went to get water at a spring. (I always thought this story was a bit far-fetched, but Dad told it so many times, I began to believe him.) It seems that when people went to the spring, this copperhead, who lived in the rocks above the spring, would come down after them—or sometimes, he would lay in wait for them, all coiled up. Dad and his oldest brother, Lloyd, heard what was going on, and they decided to eliminate the problem. Dad said Lloyd carried a shotgun and he had a lantern. They went to the spring after dark. Immediately, they heard the copperhead crawling along, rustling the leaves as he moved. Dad said he was so scared that the lantern shook, and Lloyd said, "Try to hold the lantern still!" All at once, just a few feet away, the copperhead crawled upon a rock and raised his head, looking for new prey. Lloyd fired his shotgun, ripping the snake's head off. The copperhead, Dad said, was the biggest he had ever seen or heard about. It could have caused intense pain and suffering, if not death, if it had bitten someone.

During the dog days of summer, they got very aggressive, trying to bite anyone or anything that came near. Our dogs were constantly being bitten, and although we spent a lot of playing time in the same places, none of us ever got bitten, which is very remarkable. I was struck at by copperheads, but somehow they missed a wide-open shot. As I figure, the main reason we were not bitten is that we usually saw the snake first.

Once when I was about five years old, I was chasing a mother hen, trying to catch one of her baby diddles (a tiny chicken) She went into a patch of weeds and rocks—a prime location for a copperhead. I had been following her around and around through the weeds and came within two feet of two coiled-up copperheads. I went screaming to the house. Mom said she would let my dad take care of it. That evening, he picked up a mowing blade and began cutting the weeds. He not only found the two copperheads I saw, but also about a dozen others!

One fall, I was squirrel hunting. I was looking up in a tree where a squirrel was cutting hickory nuts. I heard something rattling the leaves at my feet, but I was not thinking about anything else but keeping my eye on the squirrel—that is, until something hit my pant leg. During dog days, people used to say that snakes were blind. Maybe this was the reason he did not get his fangs in me. I looked down and saw a copperhead coiling himself up for another strike. I immediately lost interest in the squirrel, stepped back out of the snake's range and watched him a few minutes as he lifted his head up trying to relocate me. When he began crawling in my direction, I pointed my double barrel and pulled both triggers at the same time. This vaporized the snake—no pieces of him could be found.

One night, my brother and my cousin were out possum hunting with a couple of mongrel dogs we had. This was right in the middle of August. How we made it without getting snake bitten is a wonder to me. I got stung by yellow jackets about fifty times, though, when I stepped on two separate underground nests.

Both of our dogs were bitten by copperheads, one of them more than once. Brownie was his name. His head and neck were swelled up horribly. Brownie got better in a few days, though. From then on, he declared an all-out war on copperheads. He would hunt them down and provoke the snake into striking. Brownie didn't seem to care about being bitten. When the snake struck, it would be stretched out defenseless. Brownie would grab the snake by the back of his head and sling him so violently back and forth that the snake would break in two. Brownie would then proceed to tear the snake into little pieces.

Since those days, strip mining for coal has totally changed the countryside. We thought it would have bad consequences for the wildlife, but that has not been the case. After reclaiming laws went into effect, the new growth of various plants and trees, such as the autumn olive berry, has attracted all kinds of animals like deer, turkeys, and bears. Copperheads are not so plentiful as before. I just wonder what Christopher Gist would write about in his journal now.

Spot: A Great Coon Dog
Reminiscences from the Author and his Brother, Ronnie, Spot's Owner

Ronnie

Where we grew up, there were two creeks separated by hillsides steeply descending from a ridge, appropriately called Rough Ridge. Not only was it very steep on both sides, but the ground was also covered with thick laurels and rhododendrons. If you were walking down the slope of the ridge, there was a creek on the left down about a mile called Hopkins Creek. On the right side of the ridge, the roughest side, was another creek called Ritchie Branch.

In the early 1970s, there were not many raccoons in our neck of the woods, and what few there were knew every trick to shake a hound dog off his trail. What was needed was a dog with a powerful nose and a lot of intelligence. While being chased, a coon will sometimes climb up a tree, climb out on a limb, jump onto another tree, climb partially down that tree, and leap out as far as he can to the ground and keep on running. By keeping to the trees, a coon can leave a gap in his trail as much as fifty yards. I never had another dog intelligent enough to figure this trick out. Another trick that a coon can pull on a dog is to swim across a creek, pond or river and cause the dog to lose its scent. On occasion, a dog might follow a coon into a body of water and they will launch into a fierce fight. Coons have been known to wear a dog down and then climb onto the back of the dog's head and push his head under the water to drown him.

A friend of mine named Kyle was making trips to a farm near Richmond, Virginia, to hunt coons. A man named Johnny who loved coon hunting ran the farm. Kyle told me about a big red and white Treeing Walker coonhound named Spot. He was a beautiful red and white hound that looked like Treeing Walker dogs should look, except for his color. These dogs are not normally red and white. Kyle urged me to make a trip up there to see and hunt with this dog. Kyle said Spot might be for sale but at a high price. Spot really put on a show the night I arrived, treeing five coons. After a couple more trips, I became even more impressed. This dog was obviously a natural. After much haggling with Johnny, I bought him for $500.00, a big price for a dog those days.

Having been a coon hunter for about fifty years, I have hunted lots of great dogs, including world champions and state champions, but Spot proved to be the best dog ever. I have lots of stories I could tell about Spot and what an outstanding coon dog he was, but a few really hit home.

I entered Spot in many competition hunts, state and national. In some hunts, as many as four hundred plus dogs were entered. I remember once in West Virginia, I entered Spot in the Mid-Atlantic States Championship. The dogs were randomly placed in groups of four, and a guide/official scorer was assigned to each group. His job was to take the hunters to their particular area and grade the dogs on their performance. A dog would be given a certain amount of points for striking first. (*Striking* means to pick up the scent.) If he treed the coon before any of the other dogs, he scored even more points. A dog could lose points if he struck first but lost the trail or failed to tree the coon. After Spot treed two coons that the other dogs could not smell, he smelled a coon that was two miles away on the other side of the Rappahannock River. This river was about 250-300 feet wide, 3-4 feet deep, and somewhat swift. I wrapped my battery light around my neck and shoulder and waded in to find my dog. This was against the guide's order as he thought crossing the river was too dangerous. Needless to say, I got to the other side and saw the treed coon. I hooked Spot up to his leash and swam him back to where the judge and the other dogs and their owners were. Spot was the highest scoring of the hunt, but our group did not return to the starting point in time, and we were disqualified. Also, Spot lost points because none of the other hunters saw the treed coon. Because of his disqualification, Spot could not take part in the second and final night.

Some of the hunters there wanted to hunt against Spot outside the official competition because his fame was spreading. They were professional breeders with wins in state and world championships.

These owners were sure their high-powered stud dogs could outrun Spot on a trail. A lot of spectators stayed around to see what would happen. It was just an unofficial match hunt, but coon hunters love to hear their dogs run. The hunters chose a few of their best dogs to go against Spot. Spot found a trail first and he had the coon treed before the other dogs could get the track lined out.

Spot was absolutely the best dog I ever hunted with. He won many trophies for me.

I bred Spot to lots of females, and some of his offspring had the color and eyes of a bird dog. I guess that is also where Spot got his nose from; his nose was always up in the air and never on the ground. This was the reason he was such a good track dog. I take no credit for training Spot, because he needed no training. He was a very intelligent dog that knew what was expected of him—that his master wanted him to run coons and nothing else. I suppose he could have been trained to be a bear hound, a mountain lion, or even a rabbit dog. I will always cherish all fond memories that Spot left with me and with others who loved him.

Neal

Ronnie had coon-hunting fever and spent a lot of money on different kinds of hounds: Black and Tan, Bluetick, Redtick, and Treeing Walker. (At this point I need to emphasize the fact that Treeing Walkers are not necessarily the best coon dogs. I have a preacher friend who has some outstanding Black and Tans.) Ronnie also used to go on a lot of hunting trips to the flatland and swamps near Richmond, Virginia. This is where he met up with Johnny. Even average coon dogs would do pretty well in the flatland where there were many coons.

I used to wonder what would happen to a dog if it caught up to one of those big boar coons. If a dog had any intelligence, he would know not to tangle with them. I once caught a boar coon in a live animal trap. I know it does not sound possible, but the coon ripped through the heavy wire it was made of and fled back into the woods. A dog by itself would be lucky to survive the fight.

I remember the first time I saw Spot—when Ronnie first brought him home. He didn't look like all the other hounds I had seen. In the daytime he just laid in his doghouse, never barking or appearing interested in anything. When it got near dark, he didn't behave like most coon hounds do—howling and jumping like crazy when they saw someone come out of the house. He would sit quietly until he saw for sure he was going huntin'. I must admit I had my doubts because he had been able to tree coons on flatlands, but what could he do with these mountain coons that no dog had been able to handle?

The first time we took him hunting, he picked up the trail of a coon but was having a difficult time, not being used to the thick underbrush and the steep hillsides of Rough Ridge. With each successive hunt, he got better and better. The coons that had so easily fooled other dogs found that they had met their match.

I didn't go hunting much, as I didn't enjoy hunting at night, but one night in the middle of August 1972, I remember Spot treeing seven coons—an unbelievable performance! That night was also memorable because I got into two different yellow jacket nests. I remember that *very* well.

My brother entered Spot in some organized hunts. Some of the opposing dogs were long-legged English hounds, and Spot also ran against dogs that were regional and state coon-hunting champions. In other words, he was the best; he had such a keen nose, he could pick up a trail faster and could outrun any of his competition.

A good loyal and faithful dog can really get to you. There is a saying that a dog is man's best friend. They don't hold grudges or ask anything for themselves; they just want to be involved in whatever you are doing. To lose one can be very painful because a dog can become a large part of a family. One day, my mom, my younger brother, and I were going into town. We stopped by Ronnie's house, but he was not there. His wife said that he had taken Spot to the veterinarian. Spot had apparently been poisoned. Someone, probably out of jealousy, had given him a bit of food laced with a toxin. The outlook was not good. Whatever the poison was had made Spot go blind and he wasn't able to walk straight. He would stagger around; it was so pitiful to see. He lived for about two more weeks before he died. Ronnie said that when he came home from work, he immediately went over to his dog. Spot was leaning against the living room couch. His head was sagging and his eyes were glazing over. His wife told Ronnie what had happened earlier. Their two-month-old baby was lying on the couch and had somehow managed to get a little too close to the edge. She came into the room and found Spot leaning against the couch so the child couldn't fall off. Ronnie went over to his Spot and saw him take two more breaths before he died. It was like Spot was holding on, waiting for Ronnie to get home.

My brother made his way down to our house. At the time, I was still living with my mom and dad. Ronnie was in agony over losing old Spot. He asked if we would mind burying him. The next morning, my dad and I wrapped Spot in a quilt and a tarp, put him in a wheelbarrow, and took him down on Rough Ridge. We dug a hole off a point that extended out off the ridge. I guess I am being sentimental, but it seemed appropriate to bury him out in the place where his hoarse barking could often be heard at night—hot on the trail of a coon. It was a beautiful spring morning in early May. Around us birds were singing and squirrels were scampering about looking for food. They didn't have a single care, but I sure didn't feel that way because it hurt like crazy to bury this ole dog. Ronnie says that when he visits Spot's grave, it still hurts after over forty years. As for me, I have never been back to his grave.

After Dad and I finished burying Spot, we picked up our tools and just stood there a while. As we turned to go, my Dad said, "Rest well, ole hound."

www.ingramcontent.com/pod-product-compliance
Lightning Source LLC
Chambersburg PA
CBHW031205090426
42736CB00009B/796